HELLO and a HANDSHAKE

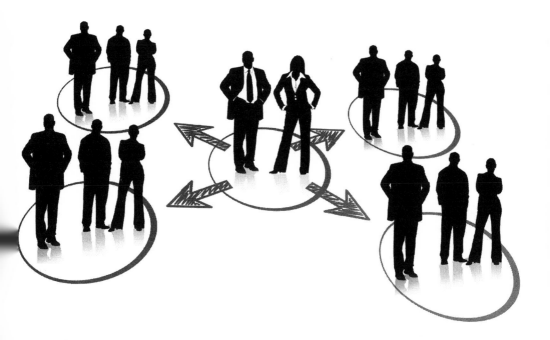

The Reluctant Networker's Guide to Survival and Success at Your Next Business Gathering

GREG PETERS

Foreword by Scott Ginsberg

The Reluctant Networker Press
www.thereluctantnetworker.com
info@thereluctantnetworker.com

Ordering Information:

Quantity sales. Special discounts are available on quantity purchases by corporations, associations, and others. For details, contact the publisher at the address above.

Printed in the United States of America

First Printing, 2017

ISBN 978-0-9988768-0-1

For my wonderful wife, Elizabeth
For standing beside me, encouraging me,
and being the love of my life.
You're a better networker than I will ever be.

ACKNOWLEDGMENTS

If you've ever been in one of my programs you've heard me say that you can accomplish nothing of real significance entirely on your own. No matter the endeavor, you had a coach, a teacher, or a mentor. You've needed a counselor, an advisor, or a confidant. You've had someone who provided encouragement, moral support, or financial support. This book is no exception. It might be my name on the cover, but those who stood with me in its creation are legion.

Another point my audiences hear is about how important it is to recognize and appreciate those who've put forth effort on your behalf. The very act of showing gratitude strengthens the connections you have.

Of course, first and foremost, thank you to my amazing wife, Elizabeth. I wouldn't be where I am without her and this book would never have seen the light of day. She has stood beside me and cheered me on when my enthusiasm ran low. She suffered through the writing, revision, and editing process with me. Many of the basic concepts of good networking I learned from her example. Never could I have asked for a better partner or love of my life than she.

Thank you to my daughters, Kaylie and Abby, who with the cats helped me to remember to have fun and not take myself so seriously. Someday they will be running the business and telling me what to do. Until then, I will take joy in watching them grow and develop networks of their own. They continue to inspire me every day with their almost natural grasp of developing great connections with those around them.

Thank you to my mom, Debby Peters, founder of Connext Nation and my personal hero. She was the first person to teach me about networking and encourage me in starting my own business. In fact, she bought me my first computer from which I ran my Web development business. Now I love that we can be colleagues in a common industry and family gatherings can be even more a meeting of minds.

Thank you to my parents, Greg and Karolyn Peters, for not smothering me with a pillow in my teenage years. I'm sure I deserved it on more than one occasion.

Thank you to my buddy Tim Householder. Of course, all of my friends have supported me in my efforts to create this book. Tim was the guy with who challenged me on every assumption I made. We spent many a late night over burgers and fries talking about connection and creativity and art. He also tested out many of the techniques I write about as he developed his own business.

Last, but certainly not least, thank you to my editor, Ken Wachsberger. He and his red pen (or the electronic equivalent) made my writing better than I ever thought it could be. I'm so glad he and I are colleagues through the National Speakers Association.

Oh, and thank you to you — for taking the time and effort to improve the world of networking, one connection at a time. See you at that next Chamber lunch!

Greg Peters, March 2017

TABLE OF CONTENTS

FOREWORD

Greg and I first connected though a hello and a handshake more than a decade ago.

We met through a mutual contact. His mother.

Talk about a positive networking introduction! She bragged about his brilliance in the way only a mother could. Kind of reminded me of my own mom, who famously tells people that she's my publicist. She works cheap.

The point is, the glowing reviews about Greg's talents weren't as biased as you might think. As we became friends and shared dinners and attended networking events over the years, one thing was apparent to me.

This guy was a total nerd. And not in that modern hipster startup quirky t-shirt wearing kind of way. But an actual nerd. As in, this guy spent his adolescence obsessed with role playing board games and other remnants of eighties pop culture.

And that's exactly why you're going to love this book. Because Greg is a master at owning his nerdy personality, unique skillset and engaging communication style to help connect others and collectively defeat the orcs of modern business.

Inside this book, you are going to learn both the principles and the practices to find and express the best version yourself, make friends and build mutually valuable relationships. But you will also be challenged to step outside your networking comfort zone. Which is a good thing. Comfortable people rarely change the world.

Read it. Take notes on it. Share it with customers. Start a book club with your team. And use it as inspiration going forward.

And remember, networking isn't about being the life at the party, it's bringing other people to life at the party.

SCOTT GINSBERG

Author. Speaker. Strategist. Filmmaker. Publisher.

Inventor. Songwriter. World Record Holder of Wearing Nametags.

THE EVOLUTION OF THE NETWORKING NERD

"Coming together is a beginning; keeping together is progress; working together is success."

~ Henry Ford

"What if you were a natural networker?"

I ask every one of my audiences this very question.

What if you felt completely confident walking into any networking opportunity? What if you were comfortable striking up a conversation with any individual or group? Wouldn't it be great if you could exchange business cards with complete strangers and somehow, magically, those little slips of paper would transform themselves into opportunities — mentors to help you steer through the challenges of your professional life, resources that would make it easier to run your business, or even clients you could serve — ones that actually pay!

Would that make a difference in your career? Would it make a difference in your life?

THE EVOLUTION OF THE NETWORKING NERD

Funny, when people see me in front of a room, working with associations, networking groups, or sales teams, they assume that I am a natural networker. I'll let you in on a little secret: Nothing could be further from the truth.

First of all, I'm not sure any such beast actually exists. Even the best networkers I know still have gaps in their approaches. Most of them freely admit to not having been particularly adept when they began their efforts at professional relationship development. Perhaps one or two are expert networkers who from their earliest years just naturally reached out to people, knew how to serve those around them without getting stepped on, and even knew how and when to ask for help. Maybe, maybe — but I was definitely not one of them. You see…

… I'm a nerd.

It's true. What many people don't know is that, before I began teaching people about the why's and how's of connecting with each other, I was a computer programmer. Do you know any computer programmers? We are not known for our outstanding social skills.

For me, though, being a programmer was a step up on the nerd continuum (see, the fact that I use phrases like "nerd continuum" should tell you just how much of a nerd I am). Prior to becoming a computer programmer, I went to school to become a mathematician. Do you know any mathematicians? I'm guessing probably not, since mathematicians make computer programmers look like social butterflies.

I've collected comic books. I played Dungeons & Dragons. Back in 2004 when my wife and I were getting married (I was in my mid- to late-thirties), my bachelor party consisted of a bunch of guys coming over to my house and playing video games. Don't think it was a complete nerd-fest, though. I think someone drank *two beers*! I know. Crazy, right?

If you got a chuckle out of that, it's okay. I'm cool with who I am, but that's not why I'm revealing my dark past. The reason I'm telling you this is so you understand the following: No matter how bad a networker you think you might be, I was much, much, much worse.

That said, I'm not letting you off the hook, because networking, believe it or not, is a learnable skill. If a socially stunted, ex-computer programmer, ex-mathematician, full-on past, present, and future nerd can learn these techniques, tools, and tactics — and be successful with them — then so can you.

So commit to the process. You can succeed.

"WAIT A MINUTE!"

I can hear you saying. "Why am I networking at all? What's the point? Why should I bother? After all, networking is just an excuse for people to leave the office so that they can eat lunch at the local Chamber of Commerce event or drink coffee with a 'leads-passing' group. I think that guy from Sales even goes out golfing and he tells the boss it's 'networking'. What use would it be for me?"

Good questions and we'll be answering them in the upcoming chapters. For now, though, I'll focus on the big one: Why would you network at all?

You undoubtedly have numerous tasks and activities in your life — items on your "to-do" list, the one that continues to grow, day by day. Think about that list and ask yourself one question:

Would these tasks be easier to accomplish with the help of someone else?

If you are trying to get more customers, would it be easier if someone else looked for those clients for you? If you are trying to serve the customers you have, would it be beneficial if someone connected you with skilled people or cost-effective resources to make you more efficient? If you are trying to find a new pediatrician, or a new school, or a babysitter for your children, would it be helpful to have someone you trust recommend them to you?

Every aspect of our lives improves when we have others that we can count on for help. Whether connecting us with prospects, resources, opportunities, teachers, decision makers, health care providers, new friends, romance, mentors, counselors, confidants, coaches, financial support, moral support, career opportunities, or fun, our network is the resource that makes it all happen. It clears the road of obstacles and allows us to grow in success and significance.

The power of our network, put simply, allows us to be the best versions of ourselves.

This book is here to help you take the first steps.

Don't be confused and think it's only to help you be more comfortable at the Chamber lunch. True, the majority of what we talk about here is about attending the formal networking event — a gathering of professionals hosted by a local business organization. In reality, a networking event is any opportunity to make contact with your fellow human beings, especially ones whom you haven't met yet. It's about first meetings, beginnings of strategic alliances, business partnerships, and professional friendships.

I've broken down the process into three sections. Part 1 looks at what you need to do to prepare for the event. As anyone who has painted a room will tell you, preparation is the most important part of the project. Skip it and the results won't look good. We'll cover the mental, physical, and informational tools you need in your toolkit.

Part 2 turns our attention to the event itself and what we can expect to experience after we slap on our nametag and walk through the doors.

Finally, in Part 3, we will cover specific tools to make you feel more confident while you are meeting potential new friends. You will learn everything from how to strike up a conversation, to how to deal with negative networkers, to how to master the all-important follow-up.

Welcome to networking. You have nothing to fear. Really, we're all friends here.

1
TURNING A NERVOUS NETWORKER INTO A COOL CONNECTOR

"One important key to success is self-confidence. An important key to self-confidence is preparation."

~Arthur Ashe

Before you delve into the mysteries of being prepared for those networking opportunities, in whatever form they might take, you first must understand what you are preparing to do. Packing your suitcase with shorts and floral print shirts probably isn't the right way to go if you are headed to the mountains for a ski vacation.

We need to take a moment to understand exactly what networking is and is not.

EVOLUTION OF UNDERSTANDING

Every networker goes through an evolution of understanding. A few simply go through it faster than others. Through our journey together, I will show you shortcuts to avoid the years of struggle I had to go through before the process began to pay off.

In general, most networkers go through three stages of networking evolution. In each stage, their practices and focus are the result of what they believe is the underlying nature of networking.

At the beginning, most people assume that networking is a sales process. Every networking opportunity is a hunt for potential clients. Those at the next stage follow the belief that networking is marketing. Here, the goal at any business gathering (or even social ones) is to inform everyone what you do and who you help. The final stage reaps the best results. At its base is the understanding that networking is a process of professional relationship development.

Here's what happens in each of these stages.

STAGE ONE: NETWORKING IS SALES

When most people start networking, they are trying to accomplish a task for which networking is not ideally suited. It's as if you picked up a hammer to pound in a screw. You might have limited success, but you end up making an ugly mess and might just hurt yourself in the bargain. You see, when most people start networking, they think they are doing so to find customers.

A person at this stage attends events with the sole purpose of making a sale. He strikes up conversations specifically to determine if anyone around him is a potential sales prospect. If he finds someone who is a perfect match — and for some that simply means that the target has a pulse — his next step is to trot out his sales script. He asks probing questions designed to make his victims feel dissatisfied with their current lot in life, which now gives the "Stage One networker" the opportunity to show how, if they buy right now, the product or service he is selling will make their lives suddenly worth living.

As you might guess, the other attendees don't appreciate someone who behaves in such a way. In fact, people shy away from him — or avoid him like the proverbial plague. He has what Debby Peters, networking guru of "Connext Nation," would call "commission breath." Let me tell you, they don't make a mint big or strong enough to take out that level of conceptual halitosis.

The problem for these would-be "networkers" is they are taking on an almost impossible task. Think about it. Selling door-to-door is a remarkably difficult job. According to those with whom I've spoken who've done it in the past, you get a belly-full of rejection in the first hour. As difficult as that is, though, can you imagine how much more difficult it would be if every time you, the salesperson, knocked on a door, the person who answered was also a salesperson who wanted to sell something to you?

Oh, and what if, while you were trying to take that other salesperson down your sales funnel, you kept getting interrupted by more salespeople from other companies who wanted to take one or both of you down *their* sales funnels? Do you think your success rate might take a hit?

If networking were simply about sales, that would be the scene at any Chamber of Commerce lunch. Those who follow this belief soon discover that networking is a frustrating task and either quit showing up — one of the top two biggest mistakes of networking — or continue showing up and making everyone around them miserable. Face it. No one looks forward to the telemarketer's phone call. They like it even less in person.

In the twenty years that I have been networking for my businesses, I think I may have sold exactly one program to someone I met at a networking event, and even that took an additional meeting after the fact.

Can you see why this isn't a particularly helpful focus for your networking efforts? Most people do. If they don't quit outright, they usually move on to stage two.

STAGE TWO: NETWORKING IS MARKETING

Once new networkers begin to suspect that the "networking is sales" mentality is not a practical pursuit, they usually hit upon a new idea. What if, instead of trying to sell to everyone they meet, they try to recruit them as their own personal sales force? After all, trying to sell to people one at a time is really hard. Far better to have each person you meet making sales for you to the people they know, right?

To this end, they start looking for an audience. They enlighten everyone they know about what it is they do and who they help. They can talk a mile a minute about the features and benefits of their products and services. This is a slight improvement over the "networking is sales" group in that they're simply trying to educate and motivate their potential sales force.

Herein lies a little truth. We definitely would like our network to be out looking for opportunities for us all the time. Here's the problem: Have you ever attended a party and found yourself seated next to that guy who talked about himself all night long? He never once showed an interest in you, unless it was to ask what you thought of him.

How did you feel about that guy? Did you want to associate with him beyond the party? Or ever again? Probably not. We have phrases to describe people like him: "self-centered," "conceited," and sometimes even just plain "selfish." None of those phrases are ones with which we want to be connected.

Here's another thought. If you've adopted this attitude, you essentially want other people to work for you — to reach out actively to their network — to bring you opportunities. You want to become a priority in their lives. How would you feel if the shoe were on the other foot? What if the Director of Business Development from a company walked up to you at a networking event and tried to convince you to introduce her to everyone in your network, to ask probing questions of your friends and relations so you could find prospects to pass back to her?

I'm just guessing, but you probably won't be inspired to rearrange your priorities.

While marketing may be a small portion of the networking process, for true networking success, we need to take one more evolutionary step to...

STAGE THREE: NETWORKING IS PROFESSIONAL RELATIONSHIP DEVELOPMENT

A few years ago, I read a great book on networking called *The Go-Giver* by Bob Burg and John David Mann. Not long after that, I met Bob in person and became a huge fan of the way he approached networking and relationship development. The way he describes networking is "the process of developing long-term, mutually beneficial, give-and-take relationships." What a great definition!

If you believe this, you are not walking into a networking event looking for prospects. You are not looking for an audience. You are looking for allies. You are looking for ambassadors. You are looking for friends.

Doesn't that change the entire approach to the networking process? Instead of viewing a connection to someone in terms of its advantage to you, you are seeking ways you can be of service to them. You start to treat them as potential friends, not targeted prospects.

You don't have to wonder what the next step is or what you should be saying. It's all about building that connection, that rapport between two people. Most of us learned how to do that in kindergarten. Working with my clientele, I've seen that the more people behaved this way, the more they looked forward to networking opportunities.

Now think about the natural results of focusing on the relationship first. If your connections see that you care about them as people, they will begin to care about you, too. When that happens, isn't it far more likely that they will tell other people about you and what you do? Isn't it more likely they will keep an eye out for opportunities, strategic partnerships, even customers for you?

In a way, if you devote your energies to the connections first, the sales and marketing just naturally fall in place

Cool, right?

So now that you know what you're preparing for, we can start by diving into the biggest block to networking success most people experience...

... what's going on inside your own head.

IN THIS SECTION YOU'RE GOING TO:

- Learn to recognize and replace a negative networking mindset.
- Make sure you're showing up at the right events.
- Identify the aspects of the networking groups that will work for you.
- Create a networking toolkit that will have you ready to connect when you walk in the door.

1

THE FIVE NEGATIVE NETWORKING ATTITUDES AND HOW TO DEFEAT THEM

"Nothing can stop the man with the right mental attitude from achieving his goal; nothing on earth can help the man with the wrong mental attitude."

~ Thomas Jefferson

Even knowing that networking is about making connections with others, a lot of people have a hard time forcing themselves to attend networking events. They have negative stereotypes of what it means to walk through the doors at a business gathering. The deck is stacked against their success before they even start.

IN THIS CHAPTER YOU'LL...

- Learn the five big Negative Networking Attitudes.
- Discover why they hurt your networking success.
- Adopt new mindsets to replace them.

A bad habit does not simply disappear. You can't just stop doing it. You have to develop a better habit to replace it. In each of the following sections I'll give you a few questions you can ask yourself to keep on the right track.

SALES FOCUS/RELATIONSHIP FOCUS

We've already touched a bit on Negative Networking Attitude number one: Having a Sales Focus. I know only a few people who truly enjoy selling. I know even fewer who enjoy being sold *to*. If your image of the local Chamber of Commerce lunch is a bunch of people running around trying to wrestle each other to the ground so that they walk out with a signed contract, well, I can understand why you wouldn't want to put yourself in the middle of *that*.

Here's the problem. Those who adopt Negative Networking Attitude number one severely limit their ability to create good connections. If you are focused only on what other people can do for you — especially if that involves giving you their hard-earned money — then any connection can only be through that narrow path. If, for instance, money changes hands or a contract is signed, then a relationship has formed. If not, the relationship has failed.

Will some people at the event see you only as a potential prospect? Yep! You'll learn how to deal with them. First, you need to address your own mental orientation. In this case, we'll replace the Negative Networking Attitude of Sales Focus with the Positive Networking Attitude, Relationship Focus.

Having a relationship focus means you will see your fellow attendees as human beings — not prospects — each with his or her own dreams, challenges, and driving passions. When you perceive this, you can connect with them on a variety of levels, not just on whether they can buy from you. As you find more common points of interest and more ways you can help them achieve what they want to accomplish, you become a more important part of their lives.

FIVE NEGATIVE NETWORKING ATTITUDES
AND HOW TO DEFEAT THEM

Then a crazy thing happens. Because you, as a person, are important to them, your *success* becomes important to them. They look for opportunities for you. Suddenly, instead of selling to one person at a time, you are connecting with potential referral partners who each might bring you several people who want to buy from you.

All because you stopped selling and started connecting.

QUESTIONS TO PUT YOU ON THE RIGHT TRACK:

1. **Do I want someone to sell at me?** If not, then don't sell at others. Reciprocity works both ways.

2. **Who would I like to meet?** This is an opportunity to meet new people. Who would build your network? Whom could you benefit?

3. **Who would I like to find out more about?** It's not always the best place to do it, but you could use this time to find out more about someone you already know.

4. **What crazy question could I ask that would show I'm not a salesperson?** It doesn't have to be bizarre, but showing a genuine interest in who they are will get you more than the most carefully crafted "elevator pitch."

5. **What questions will I ask that aren't related to business?** Always remember, you are connecting with other *people*. Most will have lives and interests outside the business world.

VICTIMHOOD/GENEROSITY

Moving on, we come to Negative Networking Attitude number two: Victimhood. It's related to the Sales Focus mindset we just talked about. This is the idea that, if you aren't careful, people will take advantage of you. Can you imagine living your life like that? Try.

Imagine you're walking into a local business after-hours' reception. It's your first event with this new group. As you enter, a smartly dressed man walks over to you with a smile on his face and his hand out to greet you. As he shakes your hand, he says, "Hi, my name is Tim. Welcome to the group!"

And your first thought is, "What does *this* guy want?"

Wow. Do you think this might put a few barriers in the way of developing new relationships? You bet it would. By the way, this was my Negative Networking Attitude back when I first started attending events; I'm speaking from personal experience.

Here's the point: This level of cynicism is unnecessary when you adopt Positive Networking Attitude number two: Generosity. The only way someone can take advantage of you is if you engage in "transactional" networking. This is the process of doing for others and then expecting them to do something for you. But if you help other people simply because it's the Right Thing to Do, with no expectation of any *immediate* return, then you are being generous.

And generosity gets repaid.

Isn't this the way friendships form outside of business? I mean, what would happen if I said to you, "I'd be happy to help you move, but I'll expect you to come over next weekend to help me paint"? Doesn't feel really friendly, does it?

Now imagine adopting the "generosity" mindset. That same conversation stops at "I'd be happy to help you move." Maybe later on,

FIVE NEGATIVE NETWORKING ATTITUDES
AND HOW TO DEFEAT THEM

I might ask if you could help me out with the painting, but I have to understand if you say "no" it's not because you took advantage of me; it's because you simply don't have time to help me.

Oh, and when "Tim" comes over to welcome you to the after-hours' reception? Your new response is, "Nice guy. I wonder how I can help him."

Not only is this a more positive frame of mind, but it's likely to be a more profitable one as well.

QUESTIONS TO PUT YOU ON THE RIGHT TRACK:

1. **What do I have to offer that no one can take away?** You have a vast storehouse of personal experience you can call on to put in the service of others. It costs you nothing and it might change their lives.

2. **Who here could I help?** Looking for opportunities to give will build a stronger, more profitable network than looking for opportunities to take.

3. **Have I met and thanked the organizers of this event?** Be generous with your gratitude and acknowledge the effort they put into making the event worthwhile.

4. **Could I pretend to be the host of this gathering?** The host mindset is one of generosity.

WORTHLESSNESS/CONFIDENCE

We've talked about changing Sales Focus to Relationship Focus and Victimhood to Generosity. Next we'll cover Negative Networking Attitude number three: Worthlessness.

A lot of the folks who attend my workshops are in transition, or, as one of my good friends, Linda Peterson of Peterson Career & Life Coaching, says, they are "between successes." Unfortunately, many people view this period as a barrier to developing the kind of powerful network they need to find that next opportunity. They believe they have nothing to offer, so why would anyone care to connect with them?

If you assume that networking is only about passing sales leads, then maybe people in transition don't have anything to offer. They wouldn't be the only ones. Heck, I've been networking for more than twenty years, and I still run into people all the time whom I could not connect with their perfect clients. That doesn't make me worthless.

I had a gentleman in one of my live seminars who was stuck in the Worthlessness trap. He felt he was new to networking and couldn't understand why anyone would want to connect with him. I took a few minutes to work with him.

After a little gentle questioning, it turned out that, while he *was* looking for a new career, he had *twenty years* of financial experience in his previous position. In addition to that wealth of business knowledge, he had put his kids through college, and had traveled extensively (and that was what I was able to find out in just a few minutes).

His incredible life experience made him a valuable connection for just about anybody. He could help people who were considering a banking career (his former position); looking for advice on dealing with their college-age children; or just seeking a good restaurant in

Maui. He might even have good advice on best practices in a job search.

All he had to do was adopt Networking Positive Attitude number three: Confidence.

We all could use a dash of confidence at times, but we especially need to remember it when we are trying to connect. Who really wants to make friends with desperation?

And here's another tip: As you continue to build your network, you become even more valuable as a resource to others. The very act of networking makes knowing you more worthwhile.

QUESTIONS TO PUT YOU ON THE RIGHT TRACK:

1. **What experiences have I had in my life that someone might like to duplicate?** You can become their advisor and guide to achieving their dreams.

2. **What experiences have I had in my life that others might wish to avoid?** Or, even better, what tools did you use to get around those obstacles?

3. **Who do I already know who helped me to achieve at a higher level in the past?** If they helped you, they might be willing to help others whom you recommend.

4. **Who could I invite to this event who might really benefit from the program?** The events you attend regularly and the groups you belong to are tools you can put in someone else's service.

DREAD/ANTICIPATION

Negative Networking Attitude number four usually results from having a few too many bad experiences at networking events. You've had one too many people shove their business card in your face. You've been trapped in boring conversations for just a little too long. Or maybe you feel like you've wasted a great deal of time and money with little to show for it. Either way, the thought of networking at an event just fills you with Dread.

Without the proper tools and techniques that response is completely understandable.

Assume you will pick up these tools and techniques as you continue to work through this book. For the moment, we will focus on the mental attitude.

When my daughter, Kaylie, was two, one of her favorite places to go in the world was playgroup. At playgroup she'd get to:

1. Meet and play with other kids.
2. Discover toys she hadn't played with before.
3. Eat a snack.
4. Have someone read a story she's not heard before.
5. Walk out with new friends she could look forward to seeing again.

Isn't that great? But what does that have to do with networking?

Think about what happens at those "dreaded" business gatherings. When you go, you get to:

1. Meet and chat with other professionals.
2. Discover ideas that you haven't considered before.
3. Get refreshments (or maybe a meal).
4. Have someone give a presentation you haven't heard before.
5. Walk out with new connections you can look forward to seeing again.

FIVE NEGATIVE NETWORKING ATTITUDES
AND HOW TO DEFEAT THEM

Listen. Networking events are just playgroups for adults! The only real difference is us. If we approached networking events with all the joy and anticipation that a toddler brings to the table, we would have a lot more fun.

Looking at business gatherings in this new light, we can replace Negative Networking Attitude number four, Dread, with Positive Networking Attitude number four, Anticipation. All we have to do is focus on the aspects of the event that fill our needs.

QUESTIONS TO PUT YOU ON THE RIGHT TRACK:

1. **What might I learn from this program?** What ideas could you learn that might make your life easier? Are you prepared to capture them?

2. **How could this event benefit my business?** Who would you like to meet? What resources could they connect you to?

3. **Who am I looking forward to *reconnecting* with?** Just because you are supposed to be meeting new people doesn't mean you can't reconnect with your existing network.

4. **Why did I choose this event or group in the first place?** You have a reason for being here. Make sure you are focused on it. Otherwise, you might end up feeling like you wasted your time.

FEELING BURDENED/PERCEIVING BENEFITS

We've come to our final Negative Networking Attitude — number five: Feeling Burdened.

I belonged to my local Chamber of Commerce for several years. When I joined, I immediately signed up for my first volunteer opportunity, the Ambassador Corps. It was our job to visit all new members and deliver their welcome gifts. I tried to make a point of staying in touch with the folks whom I had met.

One day as I was making my calls, I reached out to one of my members who had joined almost a year prior. She was happy to hear from me, but when I asked her how her Chamber membership was doing, she got quiet.

"I've decided not to renew my membership."

"Oh, okay, I know the Chamber isn't perfect for everyone. Is there a particular reason you've decided to leave?"

"Well, I'm just not getting the business I expected. In fact, I haven't gotten a single new customer from the Chamber."

I knew that her target market, local restaurants, was fairly abundant in the group. Curious, I asked:

"Hmm, well, I can definitely understand that. If you don't mind my asking, which events have you been attending?"

"Oh, I don't have time to do that!"

"Ahhhh."

What else could I say? This bright business owner let the negative attitude of Feeling Burdened get in the way of what could easily have been networking success. She felt that the time she would have spent driving to, attending, and returning from the Chamber lunches and breakfasts would be wasted and she, like so many of us, just didn't have time to waste.

FIVE NEGATIVE NETWORKING ATTITUDES
AND HOW TO DEFEAT THEM

What she didn't take into account was the lost opportunities to connect not only with local restaurant owners but with all the other Chamber members and staff who could quite easily have referred her. Would she have come home with a signed contract from every event? Nope! But she could easily have developed the relationships that would have made her investment in the Chamber pay off in the long run.

Before you let Feeling Burdened derail you from your networking success, remember Positive Networking Attitude number five: Perceiving Benefits. When you have the proper tools in hand, time spent is time invested, not wasted.

QUESTIONS TO PUT YOU ON THE RIGHT TRACK:

1. **What is taking up the majority of my time right now?** Could someone at this event connect me with a third person who could help me? Your network is more than just about getting new clients. It's a resource to connect you with opportunities to improve all aspects of your professional life (and personal, for that matter).

2. **What industries would I like to know more about?** Could someone at the event answer your questions? Maybe she could even tell you how better to serve your target customers.

3. **Is there anyone in my network who needs help?** What resources might they need? Who at this event might be able to help? Make yourself a connector.

That's the last of them. If you're resisting showing up at the networking event, take a moment right now to look at your own attitudes. Are Sales Focus, Victimhood, Worthlessness, Dread, or

FIVE NEGATIVE NETWORKING ATTITUDES
AND HOW TO DEFEAT THEM

Feeling Burdened standing in the way of your success? Adopt the Positive Networking Attitudes of Relationship Focus, Generosity, Confidence, Anticipation, and Perceiving Benefits and see how much further they take you.

2

THE THREE KEYS TO FOCUSED NETWORKING

"That's been one of my mantras — focus and simplicity. Simple can be harder than complex: You have to work hard to get your thinking clean to make it simple. But it's worth it in the end because once you get there, you can move mountains."

~ Steve Jobs

MAKING APPLE PIE

Assuming you follow the recommendations from the last chapter, you aren't the one blocking your path any longer. You have your thoughts in the right place. Now we need to make sure your body is on the right path.

What do I mean by that?

Suppose you want to make a fresh apple pie. You get out your grandma's recipe — the one that's been handed down for generations. You've got the pie pan, measuring cups, and spoons. You've gathered your spices and all the ingredients for the crust. All you need are fresh apples. You hop in your car and drive out to the nearest orchard. You grab your basket and walk out among the trees... and run into a little problem.

It's a peach orchard.

Unfortunately, even if you pick every peach off every tree, you won't have enough apples for your pie. Sometimes the nearest orchard just isn't the right orchard.

People do this in networking all the time.

They show up at a networking event or join a group and try to connect with everyone in sight. At the end of the day they have nothing to show for it because where they are isn't where they need to be. For them, the whole networking process ends up being a complete waste of time.

In fact, this leads to what is probably the number one question I get about networking events: Where's the best place to network?

If you knew this you could remove doubts. You'd know the people at the event are the ones you should meet. You wouldn't be wasting time and money on the gatherings that wouldn't benefit you. You'd even be able to justify your decision to attend these particular events or join these specific groups. After all, you probably have a boss (or a partner or a spouse) who wants to make sure that the lunch you're attending will contribute to the bottom line.

The problem is, I can't tell you the answer.

Oh, it's not like I have a big secret and I'm holding out on you just to be nasty. What I mean is, the "best" place to network is different for different people and their different goals. To answer the question for *you*, we need to take a look at the Three Keys to Focused Networking and see how they apply to your practice.

IN THIS SECTION YOU'LL...

- Develop your ultimate networking goal.
- Decide who you need to help you and where you can find them.
- Discover who can help you connect with that group.

KEY #1: YOUR NETWORKING GOAL

The First Key to Focused Networking is the answer to the question: *What is the ultimate goal you are trying to achieve through networking?* Are you trying to grow your business by finding new clients or customers? Maybe you've got more business than you can handle and you need more people to help you increase your capacity. Are you looking for employees or partners? Maybe you need subcontractors or suppliers.

Or maybe your business isn't an issue at all and you are instead trying to focus your efforts on serving a charitable organization. Or maybe your business isn't working out and now you are looking for employment. Maybe you aren't sure what you are doing and you would like to talk with a good coach or mentor.

Take a moment right now and figure this out. In fact, now would be a good time to put a bookmark on this page, close the book, take out a sheet of paper and actually write this down. Go ahead. I'll wait.

Seriously, take time to write this down or at least give it some thought. Knowing what you are trying to achieve is fundamental to success in networking.

Did you do it?

Okay, back to work. If you actually wrote down your ultimate networking goal, you now have your first key.

KEY #2: WHO YOU NEED

The Second Key to Focused Networking is quite possibly *the* most important factor in your networking practice. This is the one that, if you know it clearly and follow where it leads, will almost assure your success. It's one of the hardest steps you have to take to become an efficient and effective networker. Heck, I *teach* these concepts and *I* had problems with this one. Are you ready for it?

In the pursuit of your goal, whom do you prefer to serve?

Some people refer to this as their ideal customer or their perfect prospect. This is your target market.

Here's the first mistake people make when they try to answer that question: They define this group based on Key #1, which is what they are trying to achieve. For example, if they are trying to grow their business through selling widgets, then they say "My target market is anyone who wants to buy a widget." Unfortunately this doesn't narrow the field on your networking efforts (unless you happen to know of an Association of Widget Buyers — don't laugh, associations exist for *everything*).

The second most common mistake is being far too general: "My target market is small businesses." This is too big a group to connect with. When you talk about your target market you must be specific. Even though it feels like you are eliminating potential customers, you need to define it as narrowly as possible. Here's why:

Except around Thanksgiving, few people truly enjoy leftovers. Most dishes just aren't as good heated up the next day.

If you aren't being specific with your target market, you are basically saying you love leftovers.

I'll explain what I mean.

Suppose I have four friends who are realtors. The first specializes in commercial properties for medium-sized businesses, the second in rental units for individuals who want to expand their investment portfolios, the third in residential dwellings for small families. The fourth? If you ask him for his target market he says, "Oh, I can do anything. I'm not limited at all."

That, my friend, is a "leftover lovin'" response. The reason is, he will be last on my mind when I do hear of someone wanting to buy real estate. Even if a referral isn't a perfect match I'll tend to pass it along to a networking partner who has specified expertise that's *close* to what's needed. For example, even though my first friend told me she specializes in mid-size companies, I would give her the referral if I have a larger organization looking for multiple commercial properties.

Whatever's left? That's what fourth realtor will see. If he's lucky. The other problem with saying you can serve "anybody" is that "anybody" reminds everybody of nobody. If you don't give your referral partners specifics to remember, then they won't.

It's not because I don't think he would do a good job. It's just that all of those other folks have decided what they are good at and that is what sticks in the front of my mind.

In what area do *you* specialize?

Just in case I'm being too subtle, let me be clear.

You will never be a truly effective networker until you can state who you prefer to serve in the clearest, most detailed manner.

This is why we are spending a large amount of time on Key #2. A good understanding of your target market underlies everything in networking. At its simplest, it allows you to tell others who you want to meet. More than that, it will help define which groups you'll belong to, which meetings you'll attend, even which networking activities you'll pursue.

For example, if your particular target market is national in scope, is it going to make sense for you to look for them at your local Chamber of Commerce networking lunch? Probably not.

If your clients are primarily construction companies, should you skip the city council meeting focusing on new zoning laws? Not if you want to be perceived as a valued servant of the industry.

Spending your time working for a charity is wonderful. If, however, you are also doing it as a networking activity, wouldn't it make sense to know that your target market feels a passion for the same cause?

We all have only twenty-four hours in the day. Focusing our efforts to serve a specific group is the only way to make networking pay off in the long run.

This leads to the next step...

FINDING YOUR TARGET MARKET

When I work with clients to determine where they should be focusing their networking efforts, I take them through a process to help them find their target market. We go through these steps because if we don't, we end up with a target market that sounds like "anyone who has a heartbeat." I'll walk you through the process, focusing on potential customers. This same mechanism works, though, no matter what you are ultimately trying to achieve.

Step 1. Look to the Past.

A good place to start is to look at those with whom you've already dealt.

Make two lists. In the first, jot down the clients you've enjoyed working with in the past. Maybe they had interesting projects. Maybe you have great connections in that particular industry. Maybe the culture of the client's business supported an enjoyable working experience. Whatever the reason, as you look back over your history, write down any names that, when you read them, give you even the faintest of "warm fuzzies."

In the second list, write down the ones that were the most profitable. This doesn't only have to be about the bottom-line revenues. Maybe they came back to you again and again with new work, giving you great long-term income. Perhaps they passed your name along to others in their industry meaning you didn't have to spend time and money on marketing. Whatever it was, your association paid off.

Do you have any that are on both lists? If so, that's great. We'll focus on specific qualities they possess. If not, don't worry. You just might have to create a profile based on two or more prior customers.

Step 2. Ask Questions.

Examine those past customers. What specific traits do they have that members of your target market should possess? You might discover that your most profitable market is C-level executives in the insurance industry. Refining it further, you particularly enjoy working with female executives who have adult children.

The best way to narrow your focus is to ask questions about the group you want to serve.

Suppose your business primarily serves other businesses.

- Do you like working with particular industries or professions?
- How about their geographic location? Are they local, regional, national, or international in scope?
- How big are they? Revenue? Number of employees? Number of locations?
- What life stage are they in? Start up? Second-stage? Mature? In decline?

- What positions within the company are you trying to reach? C-level executives? Directors of Marketing? HR managers?
- Is the company going through any particular transitions right now? Are they downsizing? Were they recently acquired? Are they expanding into new markets? New product lines?

You can ask similar questions if you have a consumer-oriented business.

- Do you want to serve particular professions?
- What's their marital status? Are they single? Married?
- Do they have children? How many?
- Where do they live?
- Do they rent or own?
- How old are they?
- What are their extra-curricular activities?
- What stage of life are they in?
- Have they gone through any life transitions? Are they selling their home? Are they looking for a new job? Are they starting a business?

The more questions you ask, the more specific your target market becomes and the more focused your networking will be. Oh, and don't discount the questions that seem to be irrelevant. If you are an insurance agent, it might seem silly that your target market is dog people, until you become known as the insurance agent who specializes in dog owners. Do you happen to know how many dog owners are out there? According to the statistics I've seen, eighty million households have dogs in the United States. I'm sure a few reside near where you live and work.

As you go through this refining process keep this distinction in mind: **Your target market is the specific group of individuals with**

whom you *prefer* to work — not just those you *can* help. A chiropractor might be able to help "anyone with a spine," but he'll get better results by focusing on country club members in their sixties who golf every weekend.

Just because you've defined a narrow target market doesn't mean you'll be turning away people you *can* help who aren't in that group. It just means that you are focusing on attracting those you *prefer* to help.

One other point to consider: You will continue to refine your target market over time. You may discover that the first one you decide on may not be exactly right. It might be too general or too narrow a market to support your needs. It's fine if this happens. Even if you are wrong, you are further along than the person who is still trying to connect with "everyone."

Step 3: Find Them

You've got that narrow target market defined. Now what do you do with it? First and probably most obvious, is to find opportunities to network with members of your target market. Find organizations and events that cater to this group and become a part of that scene. Start making refinements to your processes so that you can better support them. Become interested in their particular needs as a group and as individuals within that group.

I can tell you are intrigued by this idea but I can hear you saying, "Okay, Greg, I can see how networking with my target market would be a good idea, but how do I find out where they meet?" That's an excellent question and I have two answers.

The first path you might take is to try to figure it out for yourself. Sometimes this path works effectively. If you are targeting local members of the law profession, then probably connecting with the local bar association is a good idea. In fact, you can connect with almost any professional group through their trade association.

Usually it simply takes a quick Google search to find the nearest chapters.

Sometimes, though, the direction is not obvious. What if you want to connect with Millennial professionals living in the Chicago area who own cars? That's when the second path comes in.

Ask.

If you know someone in your target market — especially if they are a past client — call them up and offer to buy them lunch. Sit down with them. Explain to them that you are trying to reach more members of this particular community and then ask their advice on where and how you can do so.

I've met few people who aren't honored when someone approaches them for advice. You are basically acknowledging them as an expert and they will almost always put forth a significant effort to help you succeed. The real benefit of this approach is that your new champion probably knows about opportunities that you would never have considered. They are more likely to be willing to invite you as their guest to an upcoming event *and* will introduce you to other members of that group.

Cool, right?

KEY #3: WHO CAN CONNECT YOU

Key #1 is all about knowing what you are trying to achieve and Key #2 is developing and refining your specific target market. Now we move on to Key #3: Knowing who can connect you to success.

"Wait a minute, Greg!" I can hear you saying. "Didn't we just do that? Isn't our target market how we connect with success?"

Well, yes, and no. Of course, connecting with your target market is a great idea. Whenever possible, you should put yourself in close proximity to this group. That way, when they are ready to buy, you are already right in front of them, ready to help. In one way, each of these connections is a potential golden egg. That's great!

But wouldn't it be nice to have the goose who could lay those eggs?

What most people fail to understand is that you develop a strong, productive network not by the number of people you know, but by the number of people *they* know. Connecting one by one with your target market is fine, but what you really want is to develop relationships with the people who can connect you with *many* members of your target market — especially those who want to buy your goods or services.

Who would be your golden goose? Consider a couple of questions:

Who else serves your target market? Who wins when you win?

Suppose you are a real estate agent whose target market is young, married professionals in their thirties with no children who are looking to buy their first home. Who else serves that market? How about loan officers at various local banks and credit unions? Relocation services might know who's coming to town. How about HR directors at large companies in the area? They'd probably know if their company was hiring, right?

A wedding photographer might want to connect with banquet halls, event planners, caterers, florists, or anyone else who works with brides-to-be. A Web developer could seek out marketing companies, graphic designers, SEO experts, printers, and user experience firms.

Of course, who you reach depends on what you do and on your target market. Basically, you want to find the group of businesses who serve your perfect customer, but don't compete with you. They tend to make good networking partners since the clients for one of you can often be clients for the other.

You'll probably agree that this is a cool idea. The trick is, how do you find them? You have three options.

First, you can guess. You might be able to come up with a fairly good approximation just by thinking about it. You'll probably miss opportunities that you might not have considered, but you should at least have a good first start.

The second option is to become an accomplished psychic and mind reader. That way you can use your supernatural powers on your current clients and unearth from whom else they buy. Let me know if you get this one to work.

Finally, you could just ask.

Just as when you were trying to find out which groups they attended, take the time to talk with members of your target market. Tell them that you would like their help in brainstorming on this idea. In particular, you want to find out who else they buy from. Most people will be more than happy to help.

Here's the point of Key #3: Find out where you can meet these Success Connectors. How? That's right. Meet or ask to be introduced to one or two of them and then ask them (just like you did with your target market).

Remember, assuming you have taken the time to build a strong connection, the people in your network (including your clients) are going to be happy to assist you in any way they can. Take the time to tap into that network to help you find others who serve your target.

As a result of going through the three Keys of Focused Networking, you now have two general categories of events and groups you should be attending:

- Those that contain your target market.
- Those that contain those who can connect you with your target market.

In general, any event you are considering attending should fall into one of these two categories.

If it isn't, then you're trying to bake an apple pie with the fruit from a peach orchard.

A FINAL REMINDER: THIS IS HARD

Seriously, if you are able to perceive the benefits of selecting a target market and stick with it, I congratulate you. You have just completed one of the most difficult tasks in networking. At first, most of the professionals who come to me have a hard time accepting the necessity of this step. After going through this process, though, they find that their networking yields better results than it ever did when they tried to focus on "anyone with a heartbeat." They attend fewer events and consequently waste less time and money.

Speaking of those events, now that you know why you are going, the next step is to determine which ones are right for you.

3

JOIN THE GROUP.
JOIN THE SUCCESS.

"As you navigate through the rest of your life, be open to collaboration. Other people and other people's ideas are often better than your own. Find a group of people who challenge and inspire you, spend a lot of time with them, and it will change your life."

~ Amy Poehler

WHO'S THROWING THE PARTY?

No discussion of networking opportunities would be complete without talking about the groups and associations that run such events for their members and for the community. At one time your choices of where to network were limited. You could join your local Chamber of Commerce. You could join the local service organization such as Lions, Elks, or the Rotary. Maybe your trade association had a nearby chapter. You may have belonged to a house of worship. That was about it.

Times have changed.

If you look at the business calendar of any decent-sized town, not a week will go by without at least one or two gatherings (both professional and social) where you could potentially network. All of these events have groups behind them — some more traditional and structured than others. In fact, if you'd like to investigate just how many groups are near you, go to Meetup (www.meetup.com) and look up your town in their listings.

As of this writing, over *two hundred* groups and clubs are located within five miles of Ann Arbor, Michigan, where I live. The focus of interest ranges from business matters, to SCUBA aficionados, to video game geeks. I even saw a group for "Bronies" (adult, male fans of the "My Little Pony" cartoon). That's just what's in Meetup. It doesn't cover the plethora of referral-passing groups, professional associations, and local Chambers of Commerce that weren't listed.

So how can you make this overabundance of groups work to your advantage? Do you even need to join in the first place?

IN THIS SECTION YOU'LL...

- Learn the many reasons you might join a particular group.
- Pick up other factors that might affect your decision to join.
- Discover the wide variety of potential groups and their respective strengths and weaknesses.
- Understand the limitations of group associations.

WHY JOIN?

Believe it or not, making sales isn't the first or best reason to join a group. If you decide to go in with only that reason in mind, your fellow members will sense your ulterior motives and, depending on how annoying you are in your selling efforts, will start to avoid you. Like the proverbial plague. Before joining any group, you need to understand *why* you are doing it. Consider these other reasons for becoming an active participant in a group.

1. **Support the organization's mission.** Every group has a reason for existing. Maybe it's to support a particular charity or underserved segment of society. Possibly they focus on policy or governmental issues affecting a particular trade or industry. They may even have a mandate to support members of the association through business development support, or maybe everyone is really into making quilts. Whatever the reason, before you join this particular group, you must, must, must support that mission. Anything less than your wholehearted belief in what the group is trying to achieve is nothing more than a self-serving and hypocritical move.

2. **You have a lot to offer.** Your annual dues and any fees you have to pay to attend meetings are just your ticket to ride. Closely related to supporting the mission, you have a lot to offer the group. What personal skills or resources could you put at the group's disposal? Do you have time to serve on the Board? Could you volunteer as an officer? Could you bring in guests on a regular basis? Whatever it is, having your skillset, time, talent, or perspective to offer the group is a necessary part of being visible to and appreciated by your fellow members, which leads to reaping greater benefits from your membership.

3. **Education.** Many groups, as a part of their regularly scheduled meetings, bring in experts with industry knowledge, business advice, or even motivational presentations to educate and engage their membership. For professions that require continuing education, these meetings serve as credit toward those requirements. In addition to the formal

offerings, though, don't forget about the opportunity to mix and converse with colleagues in your industry or peers in the business world. Most of the time they are more than willing to share best practices that could make your challenges more easily overcome.

4. **Fun.** Networking doesn't have to be all work. Groups actually have enjoyable social events. Why not attend one that interests you? When I belonged to the Ann Arbor Chamber of Commerce, they had gatherings at a local skeet shooting facility, at a nearby race track, and at a college football game. Different groups might have end-of-year parties, golf outings, or summertime picnics. Of course, those are just the business-oriented organizations. Other groups get together specifically for enjoyment. Whether it's a hobbyist group for quilting, a sports team, or a book club, the focus may be on entertaining the participants, but they are still excellent networking opportunities. Look for those opportunities and have fun!

5. **Discounts and other benefits.** Yeah, it may not be sexy, but joining an organization to get access to discounts on various goods and services is perfectly valid. Many Chambers of Commerce offer lower prices on insurance, Internet service, and office supplies. Our local Chamber maintains a catalog of member-to-member discounts. This is all good. Be aware, though, when you are looking to join a group to meet a specific segment of the membership. If they joined only to get discounts, they might not actually be showing up for networking events. Always attend a few meetings first to make sure the "active" members are the ones you want to meet.

6. **Social interaction.** Especially for those of us who are sole proprietors, solo-preneurs, freelancers, or otherwise work

by ourselves, our day-to-day lives can get a little lonely. Becoming part of a larger group can help alleviate these feelings of isolation, especially if the group in question caters to those whom we consider our peers. This was especially true for me when I joined the National Speakers Association. Many people in my life don't actually understand my occupation, but my fellow speakers do. They really get what motivates me to stand up in front of a crowd of strangers and talk. In fact, when a new member joins the group, they are often greeted with the phrase "Welcome Home!"

7. **Referrals.** There's nothing wrong with joining a group to receive more referrals. We just have to be careful that we don't have that as our sole motivation. Even in so-called referrals-passing groups, you have to bring your own resources to the table to benefit other group members. If you are only there for yourself, your fellow members will sense your self-seeking intentions and will start to avoid you. No one likes to be used or even suspect that's the case.

The groups you consider joining will depend on which of these benefits you want to enjoy. Different groups will have strengths in different benefits. Be aware of your own motivations and you will be more likely to achieve success.

POINTS TO CONSIDER BEFORE JOINING THE GROUP

The benefits you will gain from being a member of the group aren't the only factors to consider when looking for networking opportunities. Several other factors may make a group more or less appropriate for your needs. Consider the following:

1. **Cost.** To become a member of most groups, monetary costs are involved. Of course you may have to pay annual dues,

but don't forget to figure in fees to attend meetings. The organization typically needs to charge a registration fee to offset the costs to run the events. On top of that, you may want to consider any additional fees that might crop up. Do you want to be more visible within the organization? Consider sponsoring an event. Just remember to figure in those additional costs to being part of the group.

2. **Frequency.** How often does the group meet? Can you show up that often? Is it often enough? Many of us are busy living our lives and running our businesses, so you'd think that a group that meets less often would be a great fit. If it meets too infrequently, though, the members may not be as tightly connected as you want. Sometimes small groups that meet less often are in danger of evaporating entirely. If you have a group of only fifteen or twenty that meets every other month, all it takes is one meeting where, for one reason or another, most members don't show up. After that, the group will see a rapid decline in participation and eventually no one will show up at all.

3. **Time commitment.** Success in a networking group is largely a factor of active and engaged participation. You can't simply sign up and expect the benefits to come rolling in. That's like buying a fishing license and expecting the fish to suddenly end up in your refrigerator, cleaned and ready to eat. You have to put in the work first. How much time can you devote to this group? How long are the meetings? Remember that, for others to see you as an active member of the group, you will have to attend most of the events and meetings associated with the group.

4. **Opportunities to serve.** Regular meetings aren't the only way you will invest your time in an organization. Look for opportunities to contribute your time and effort in service.

As I mentioned back in Chapter 1, when I joined the Ann Arbor Chamber of Commerce, I asked the membership director what volunteer positions were available within the Chamber. She connected me with the Ambassador Corps. This group acted as hosts for the regular networking events and acted as the "welcome wagon" for new members. We met with new members of the Chamber to help orient them and educate them on the many benefits of membership. It took a little extra time — two or three hours per month — but ended up making a big difference in the results I saw from my membership. Holding that service position meant that I was more visible to the membership at large. More importantly, I was more strongly connected to my fellow Ambassadors. In fact, one of the Ambassadors referred me to one of *his* clients that resulted in one of my largest contracts at the time. Sometimes being a member of a smaller, visible subgroup means you are more visible to the larger main group.

5. **Group makeup.** Who are the members of this organization? Are they the ones you need to meet? If you are trying to make more sales, you probably want to make sure members of your target market are a part of the group. If you would like more referrals, you need to make sure your Success Connectors are a part of the group. If you are looking for moral support and best practices, then you probably need to see your industry colleagues on the membership rolls.

6. **Who shows up?** Just because a group claims that it has your target market as members doesn't mean it's a good match. Sometimes people join groups not for the networking events, but rather for the discounts or other benefits the group offers. There's nothing wrong with that, but if you joined the association to meet small business owners and

instead all you are seeing are salespeople at the business gatherings, you might need to reconsider whether this is the right group for you.

7. **Membership engagement.** Before you commit to a particular group, attend several of its gatherings. How engaged are the members? While you want opportunities to serve, a serious red flag is if every subcommittee is desperately looking for volunteers. If the group has two thousand members, that's all well and good (assuming that's what you are looking for), but if only fifty of them are showing up at the programs, that can reflect a membership that has started taking the benefits for granted. The size can indicate its chances for longevity, but the number of people who show up is a better indicator for your personal success.

8. **Leadership engagement.** Sometimes people become leaders of a group for the wrong reasons. Whether it's ego or sales or even simply an unwillingness to say "No," a leadership team that isn't focused on actively pursuing the benefit of the group can be a crippling factor in the success of the organization. Is the leadership visible? Are they planning new efforts to grow and strengthen the group? Do they even know and understand their current plans?

9. **Presence of guests.** Are new people showing up to check out the program? Are the members so excited about this group that they want to spread the word to everyone they know? Not seeing guests at every event (at least those open to guests) is a another red flag on the group's long-term health. Even the strongest organizations have turnover. People retire, are promoted to different positions, move to different locations, or otherwise have changes in the seasons of their lives. It's sad when members leave the group, however, if new members are joining continually, the group will likely

persist and thrive. If not, your networking prospects shrink and the group may find itself shutting down.

TYPES OF GROUPS

Now you have a handle on the different benefits you might receive from being part of a group. Next, consider the different types of groups you could join and which of those benefits might come into play for each.

TRADITIONAL

Otherwise known as open groups, this category covers local Business Associations, Chambers of Commerce, and other general business organizations. Most of the members will be entrepreneurs, professionals, or employees of local businesses. Joining is relatively easy and rarely involves restrictions. Most people think about "traditional" groups when they think of business networking groups. Usually, these groups are focused geographically and, in fact, often have that region incorporated in their name — the Motor City Jaycees, the Howell Area Business Association, and the Bay City Area Chamber of Commerce. Depending on the mix of businesses in the area, the group may have a bias toward a particular category of member (insurance, manufacturing, technology), but it isn't necessarily the mission of the group to support that particular sector. They are, almost by definition, generalists.

You benefit since you are likely to find a representative of almost any type of person or business. Depending on the size of the group, you could run into everyone from front-line staff to business owners to company executives. The downside is you might have a challenge even locating them in the crowd. Heck, the other members might have a hard time locating *you* in the crowd.

One way around this with larger groups is to find a smaller subgroup or committee where you can serve. People who volunteer to work for the organization tend to be better networkers. They recognize that the benefits they want to achieve through their membership come about as a result of a deeper level of participation.

The larger groups in this category will often have many different types of events going on over the course of a month. These might include breakfast business card exchanges, lunch-and-learns, business after-hours gatherings, seminars, workshops, and social events. The downside is you could easily fill up your networking calendar with event possibilities from just this one group. Before you do, be aware that each event will have its own "character", made up of the types of members who tend to show up. For example, when I was attending Ann Arbor Chamber of Commerce meetings regularly, the morning programs were the "suit set" — mostly executives and business owners — who wanted to get in their networking before their work day started. The lunchtime programs tended to have more sales reps, financial advisors, real estate agents, employees, and those who were representing network marketing companies such as Amway and Mary Kay. Evening events tended to attract a younger crowd, especially those who were single or had no children — often at the beginning of their careers.

You'll want to be aware of these different characteristics so you attend those events that serve those whom you are trying to meet. No point in joining a group if you don't have those opportunities.

Traditional groups potentially have numerous other benefits, including, for instance, marketing opportunities, educational seminars, and discounts. When you talk with the person in charge of membership, be sure to get the entire list of resources at your disposal as a member.

Advantages:

1. You can connect with a diverse membership of businesses and individuals.

---

2. The group offers many visible opportunities to serve your fellow members.

3. You can attend a variety of event types at different times of day.

4. Services and educational opportunities help with your business or career.

5. The organization may offer members-only discounts on local goods and services.

Disadvantages:

1. Depending on size, it's easy to get lost in the crowd.

2. Networking can be unfocused because of the wide variety of members.

3. Annual and per-event costs can get expensive.

Tactics:

1. In larger groups find smaller subgroups.
2. Volunteer to serve in a visible position.
3. Attend all meetings.
4. Invite guests.
5. Verify that the active members are the ones with whom you want to network.

SERVICE CLUBS

Service clubs, such as Rotary International, Kiwanis, Elks, Lions, Exchange, Optimist International, and others have many of the same qualities as traditional business networking groups. They have regular meetings. The membership can come from a variety of backgrounds. A plethora of opportunities are available for active, visible participation.

But while the traditional group focuses on business, the service club has a specific mission to serve the community. In fact, in certain service groups, it's considered bad form to discuss business at all. That said, the only restriction on joining most of these groups is that you support their mission. Even that probably isn't strictly required, but you shouldn't join a group whose mission you don't support wholeheartedly. Anyone who does is hoping to develop relationships based on a deception. Not the best way to start a healthy network.

Assuming you're committed to supporting the mission of the group, the best way to make your membership pay off is — as with traditional networking groups — find a visible way to serve. At the minimum, of course, you will need to volunteer your time to the various service activities the group organizes. These could range from helping the homeless to planting trees in a local park to teaching people how to read. Be aware the group may also have certain financial expectations of its members, both in straight donations and in other forms of fundraising.

Advantages:

1. Members come from a variety of businesses and from all over the community.
2. Service clubs attract decision makers and centers of influence as members.
3. Everyone in the group has a shared interest, which makes connecting easier.

Disadvantages:

1. Time and financial commitment are higher than in general networking groups.
2. Some groups have cultural taboos about discussing business.

Tactics:

1. Understand the expectations of membership and be willing to accept them.

2. Attend all meetings.
3. Find visible ways to support the group. Volunteer.
4. If you wish to connect with specific people, make sure you volunteer for what they do.

TRADE ASSOCIATION (YOURS)

If you have your own business, many people will tell you to join your trade association. I agree. Just don't join it expecting to get new clients, because it's unlikely to happen.

As a professional speaker, trainer, and consultant, I joined the National Speakers Association several years ago. Since that time, I have received precisely two pieces of business from another member of the group.

Two.

It's not that they aren't willing, but, guess what? They are all looking for business, too. This is going to be the case for any trade association. Why bother joining?

Clearly, for a few occupations, you don't have a choice. As a lawyer, you have to be a member of the American Bar Association. Medical doctors? The AMA. In fact, almost any practice that calls for a certification will require that you join a trade group. Often that certification comes with an additional "continuing education" requirement that the association works to satisfy. They organize regular meetings where speakers present information on the latest changes in the industry, new regulations that might affect your business and general business practices and techniques (like networking) designed to make you better able to compete and succeed. Even for those of us who don't need the letters after our names, those educational opportunities can make good sense.

The biggest benefits, though, come from being surrounded by a group of your peers and colleagues. These are the folks who are doing what you are doing. They understand the challenges you face and may already have faced and overcome them. They can be a source of great information on best practices in the industry. At the very least, they can provide a sense of community, which helps alleviate that feeling of isolation that many business owners can experience.

Advantages:

1. You become a member in a community of like-minded individuals who understand the challenges of your industry.
2. The group provides educational opportunities to further specific industry awareness or general business skills.
3. You may receive some referrals.

Disadvantages:

1. Membership is unlikely to generate significant business.
2. Some trade associations can be expensive.

Tactics:

1. Approach this group with the purpose of finding support in your business, either through educational offerings, connection with others in the industry, or a combination of the two.
2. Attend regularly.
3. Look for non-members who would benefit from the group and might be potential members.

TRADE ASSOCIATIONS (NOT YOURS)

Joining your trade association can be a good idea, just not for the purposes of getting clients. If you are hoping for those, then the industry group you want is probably the one associated with your target market. Wait, you think you can't join because you aren't in the industry? You might not be, but you do *serve* that industry, right? If you want to *serve* that market segment better, you had best become aware of the challenges they face. Joining their trade association is a great way to do this.

In fact, many trade groups have affiliate memberships just for someone like you. By joining under this category, you are officially a part of their association and now you can find out what the needs of this group really are. And right after you join you should start passing out your business card and asking everyone you meet whether they want to buy from you. Right?

Wrong.

In fact, this is the exact opposite of what you should be doing. Many trade members look askance at affiliate members specifically because they are waiting for the hard sell. They believe the affiliate is only a self-serving member — there for his own benefit — and so they avoid him because they don't want to hear the sales pitch. Who would?

To make an affiliate membership work for you, you first have to show yourself as a true servant of the group. Look for any opportunity to volunteer. Can you sponsor a meeting or other event? Can you find solutions to the challenges the group (or individuals within the group) is facing — solutions from which you don't necessarily gain benefit? If you can show yourself to be supporting the organization in every interaction, then you can develop the strong relationships within the group. It's those relationships that will connect you with opportunities and potential new clients.

Advantages:

1. You are surrounded by members of your target market.
2. You have the opportunity to learn about specific challenges that you might be able to meet.

Disadvantages:

1. Because you don't work in the industry, other members may view you with suspicion.
2. Time commitment may be higher because of the need to volunteer.
3. Monetary costs may be higher both for membership and for sponsorship opportunities.

Tactics:

1. Focus on relationships and service first, active prospecting a distant second.
2. Volunteer, volunteer, volunteer.
3. Ask industry members how better to serve the industry. Let them become your unofficial advisory board.

ALUMNI ASSOCIATION

If you attended college, consider joining and participating in your alumni association. The primary focus of these groups is to bring together those with a shared history at an institution of higher learning and foster those connections between the members. Most alumni groups have regular gatherings — meetings, seminars, and other educational opportunities, of course, but also activities for just plain fun. My wife belongs to the Alumni Association for the University of Toledo. Through that membership, we've attended ice skating/pizza parties, concerts with the Toledo Symphony Orchestra, and even a ski trip up north. Each year they arrange a chartered plane trip to support the football team in whatever bowl game they happen to be playing.

The events aren't the only benefit you should consider. Many alumni associations give members access to discounts on insurance, prescription drugs, travel, cars, and technology purchases. If you think you might be investing in any of these, you could easily make up the cost of membership with savings from these group benefits.

As if that weren't enough, let's talk about the networking. The folks who join these groups often are quite successful in their careers already. Many of the people I've met at events are nearing retirement and are more than happy to be mentors. They've achieved success, now they want to leave a legacy. They often happen to be highly connected in the community and fully understand the value of sharing those connections.

The downside here is that the networking might be a little unfocused. If you are trying to make connections with a particular market, you may have to meet a lot of people at the general events to find the ones you are seeking. That said, especially in the larger universities, specific schools may have subgroups within the larger association. Law, medicine, engineering, and other departments often sponsor their own events, which, while open to the general membership, tend to have a higher concentration of particular industries represented.

Advantages:

1. Membership is relatively inexpensive — usually considerably under $100/year.
2. You have access to a variety of events.
3. Making connections can be easier because you already have shared experiences.
4. For larger institutions, almost every state will have a chapter.
5. Most associations offer discounts and other benefits.
6. Members are often already successful in their careers.

Disadvantages:

1. Networking can be unfocused due to general nature of membership.

2. Events can be costly.
3. Limited opportunities for volunteering means becoming visible requires more effort.

Tactics:

1. Verify that the group with whom you are trying to connect is actually represented within the association.
2. Find and attend the events that appeal to you and bring you in contact with your target group (or those who can make introductions to same).
3. Take advantage of any benefits that might help defray the costs.

SOCIAL/RECREATIONAL GROUP

Are you a member of a quilting circle, a book club, a wine-tasting group? These — and any other gatherings devoted to pursuing a common social or recreational purpose — are all networking opportunities. A good friend of mine, a financial advisor at a boutique firm, was a former college basketball player. She still loves to play and goes out to the local gym fairly often to play pick-up games. While there, she networks with her fellow players — often well-to-do professionals in the area — who could easily make use of her services.

Social groups can be marvelous ways to connect with those around you. You all share a common interest, which can go a long way toward making those first conversations easier. Plus, since this isn't a business-oriented venue, people act more like themselves. In addition, you are less likely to have someone selling at you. To put it simply: They're fun!

The downside of these groups is that they *aren't* focused on business. If you are joining for the specific purpose of pursuing customers, you may be disappointed. As we talked about earlier, though, increasing your bottom-line isn't the only reason to join a networking group. These types of organizations tend to fulfill those other reasons.

Advantages:

1. Casual atmosphere and common focus make meeting new people easier.
2. Because the group isn't business-oriented, other members are less likely to sell at you.
3. Groups are often inexpensive or even free to join.

Disadvantages:

1. Because the group isn't business-oriented, any sales results will likely be incidental at best.

Tactics:

1. Join these groups because you share the common interest and want to share it with others.
2. Focus on the fun and the relationships.
3. Don't expect business unless your target market includes those who pursue this interest.

LEADS/REFERRAL PASSING

One of the most popular types of networking organizations for business development is the Leads/Referral Passing group. Business Network International (BNI) is the largest and most successful of these. A number of local and regional groups belong in this category, too. Local Business Network, Power Through Networking, and CaerusNet are just a few of the ones around Ann Arbor. Often Chambers of Commerce will offer this service to members. These organizations each have their own rules, frequency of meetings, and specific agendas. Underlying them all, though, are two concepts:

JOIN THE GROUP. JOIN THE SUCCESS.

1. **The goal is to exchange (give and receive) business opportunities with other members of the group.** You are expected to be actively looking for referrals for the other members. Some groups will even give you a scorecard based on the number of referrals you pass out to the other members.

2. **They are usually a "closed" networking group.** In other words, any given local chapter has only one representative from any given industry.

Obviously, this group is extremely business oriented. They want their members to succeed and the most successful groups are constantly working to train their members on how best to accomplish those goals. With few exceptions, these groups are self-facilitated, which means ample visible opportunities to serve — everything from acting as a greeter, to setting up coffee, to actually running the meeting as an officer.

One downside of being a member of a referrals-passing group is (as mentioned), you are expected to connect your fellow members to business opportunities. That's fine, so long as you believe they are skilled at the services they offer. If you aren't sure about the quality of their work, though, it can lead to awkward situations where you don't want to pass along the people you know because it might damage *your* reputation. This is why it's especially important to maintain strong connections within the group. That means, in addition to the regular meetings, you should be getting together with the other members for one-to-one opportunities — coffees and lunches.

Some people aren't comfortable with the meeting formality and the leads-passing requirements. Understand, though, if you have a business that benefits from these types of connections, then one of these groups could be a real win for you. If you are considering becoming a member of a particular group, take the time before joining to see whether the "personality" of the group is going to mesh with yours.

JOIN THE GROUP. JOIN THE SUCCESS.

A few years ago, I joined one of these organizations. I attended a couple of times as a guest and they seemed friendly. They only met once a month, which seemed like a schedule I could keep. I filled out the application and started attending. It started slowly — not many (not *any*, actually) referrals for me. I met with several members, none of whom could see how to help me. Still no referrals. I gave my ten-minute presentation. Still nothing. That's when I discovered all the little details I should have been watching for when I was still a visitor. So that you don't experience the same frustrations and lack of results as I did, here are questions you should be able to answer in the positive before you find a seat at the table.

1. **During the thirty-second commercials (or member education minutes or whatever they call them) are attendees taking notes?** If they aren't, then it isn't likely that they will be able to pass good referrals. In fact, if they aren't taking notes, they will usually forget about the needs of the other members sometime between getting their last cup of coffee and walking to the car after the meeting.

2. **Do other members share your target market?** If they don't, it won't be easy for them to refer to you nor you to them. In general, if it isn't easy, it probably isn't going to get done.

3. **Is the meeting frequency both one you can commit to and one that will be productive?** The group I joined only met once per month. That was a schedule I could maintain for the most part. Unfortunately, it wasn't often enough to generate any results. From other groups I've visited, the minimum frequency to still see good referrals passing is every two weeks. If meetings are any further apart, it's hard to keep the need for finding referrals in mind. Remember, too, most groups have an attendance policy. If you sign up, you must show up.

4. **Is the size appropriate?** If the group has less than twenty members — unless it is just starting out and still in its rush of growth — it's likely to be dying off. On the other hand, if it has more than fifty members, you could get lost in the shuffle.

5. **Are people passing referrals?** It's kind of the whole point of this group. How effectively are they passing referrals to each other? You should ask them for their statistics and observe during the meeting. Remember liars can figure and figures can lie. If they say they've had hundreds of referrals passed in the last year that means they may have passed as few as four referrals per week. If they have thirty members, is that the level of activity you want? When it comes time to pass referrals, how often do you hear the phrase "I'll keep you all in mind"? That's a real danger sign because, for the most part, they won't.

6. **Do many guests attend?** If you don't see one to three other guests each time you attend the normal meetings, it's a sign that the group might be starting to fail. How many members did they have last year? How many regular attendees? How many this year? Is that number up or down? If they don't have guests, they don't have new members to replace the old ones who moved on for one reason or another.

7. **Does the expected return justify the expense?** It costs money to join and participate in these organizations. Usually they have an annual fee often in the hundreds of dollars. Then most will have a per-meeting fee to cover costs of the location and any refreshments they might have. They might have additional fees for materials and training. Total up all of this; then look at how many referrals you would have to receive in order to break even and whether that is even likely to happen.

One caveat on all these questions: Remember that, as with any networking group, it takes time and persistence to develop the kind and depth of relationships that you need to receive the referrals you want. Depending on your business and the perceived risk of referring to you, it could be as long as a year before you start seeing significant results from your efforts. Be aware of that before you give up on groups like this too soon.

Advantages:

1. These groups are business oriented. The purpose is for members to pass referrals to each other.
2. The structure of the group promotes developing deeper relationships.
3. You may have opportunities for additional networking training.
4. Each group limits membership to one from any given industry — no competition within the group.

Disadvantages:

1. Attendance can be time demanding. The group expects you to attend every meeting or find a substitute.
2. Meetings often (but not always) take place early in the morning.
3. Membership fees and per-meeting fees can get expensive.
4. As a requirement of membership you should bring referrals to each meeting.
5. Because the group limits membership to one from any given industry, you may be locked out of a given chapter.

Tactics:

1. Be particularly careful selecting the group. You will be spending significant time, effort, and money on them.
2. When you join, start meeting with other members right away. Meet to form better relationships and learn about how you can help each other.

LIMITS TO MEMBERSHIP

As you can see you have numerous types of groups you can join for the purposes of networking. You simply need to understand what benefits you want to achieve and find out what available organizations fit those needs.

One last caution: Don't try to join every group in your area.

I've had clients who tell me that they're burnt out on networking. That's usually a red flag for me. When I ask them what groups they belong to, they'll give me a laundry list of multiple Chambers of Commerce, several trade associations, a variety of service or charitable organizations, and even one or two social/recreational groups. Whew! I get exhausted just listening to their list. I can only imagine what it's like for them to have every minute of their professional (and personal) lives taken up by event after event after event.

Here's the rule: In networking, better to go deep than to go wide.

You want to belong to only a few groups where you can make a real impact. Remember that it's not enough simply to join. You need to form real relationships with your fellow members. That means you need to devote time, energy, and money — resources we each have only in finite supply. For most people, actively participating in three groups is sufficient to gain the results they want without risking "Networking Burnout."

Speaking of these groups and the events they sponsor, now that you know where you are going, the next step is to go there. What could be easier? I mean, you might as well put this book back on the shelf right now.

Wait. What's that? You still aren't one hundred percent comfortable with attending the networking event? If that's the case, let's do a little preparation so you can start strong.

CHAPTER

4

PREPARING EFFECTIVE TOOLS FOR BUILDING POWERFUL CONNECTIONS

"The expectations of life depend upon diligence; the mechanic that would perfect his work must first sharpen his tools."

~ Confucius

To succeed in any task, you must have the right tools. If you want to dig a hole, getting out a feather duster probably isn't going to help. Likewise, using your bare hands, while do-able, isn't going to be an efficient way to go. Networking is no different.

When attending a business gathering, I recommend three different categories of tools to gather: physical objects, event information, and mental preparation. We're going to dive into each of these so that your toolbox is complete and ready to go the moment you are.

PREPARING EFFECTIVE TOOLS FOR BUILDING
POWERFUL CONNECTIONS

IN THIS SECTION YOU'LL...

- Learn the importance of properly timed preparation.
- Create your physical, mental, and informational networking toolkit.
- Develop the replacement for your "elevator pitch."

Before you start learning about these, though, you must follow one rule if you really want to be successful:

PREPARE THE NIGHT BEFORE

Trust me. I know about this.

Several years ago, my good friend and sales coach, Joe Marr, invited me to attend a seminar on negotiating that he was presenting at 10 a.m. on a Monday morning. I'm thinking *10 a.m.? Great! That means I don't have to get ready the night before. After all, 10 a.m. is extremely late in the morning that I should be able to take care of everything after a good night's sleep.*

Please note the horribly flawed assumption in that thought.

Sure enough, we had a "complicated" evening on Sunday night with our daughter, Abigail, who was three at the time, and I over-slept until after 9 a.m. You can imagine what happened next. I was flying around the house, trying to shower and shave, searching out my networking outfit, looking for my materials, not finding my materials, and so on, and so on.

What was the end result?

First, I was rushed. Rushing around creates stress. I was off balance and not in my best networking frame of mind.

I did arrive on time. Barely. Some would think that this was okay, but what this actually meant was that I arrived just in time for the presentation and had no time for networking.

Other than a quick hello, I missed chatting with Joe. Joe serves the same folks as I do and we don't really compete. That means we can easily refer business to each other. Fortunately, we already have a well-established relationship, but it never hurts to touch base and I missed out that day.

Here's the big one. I missed an opportunity to connect with members of my target market. As I said, because Joe serves the same people as I do, the rest of that packed room fell into my target market. No, I didn't think I was going to walk out with a signed contract or anything, but networking with potential prospects is always a good idea — assuming I'd get there in time to do so.

Another factor that threw me off was I didn't have my materials. I couldn't find my business card holder. I forgot my pen and notebook. I didn't have my watch. I even forgot my cell phone. You know that dream where you are still in school? In the dream, you walk into class and realize that they're having an exam? Then you realize that you're completely unprepared because you haven't attended a single lecture all semester? You know that dream? That's how I was feeling.

Here's my recommendation. Each evening, before you close up shop (whenever that is for you), look through tomorrow's schedule. If you have any sort of networking going on, pretend it starts at 6 a.m. and prepare accordingly. Don't assume you can get it together the next day, because sure as shootin' something will sooner or later get in your way.

Now that we've covered that, here are the physical tools you'll need to be successful and less stressed.

THE PHYSICAL TOOLS

When I present my live, in-person "Creating Connections with Success" programs I ask participants what they think is the most important physical object to have in their networking toolkit.

PREPARING EFFECTIVE TOOLS FOR BUILDING
POWERFUL CONNECTIONS

Almost without fail the first answer is "business cards." After that they'll occasionally throw in "the agenda," "your nametag," and "a smile." While all of these objects are important to have, in my opinion, none of them is *the* most important.

Given that one of the primary reasons you attend a networking event is to meet new people with whom you will follow up, the number one tool is... **your schedule.**

If you meet someone with whom you want to explore a long-term professional relationship, you can plan your next meeting with them before you even leave their presence. It will save you one more step in the networking process. Whether on a smart phone or in a day planner, many people carry their schedules with them these days, so it makes it easy to set up that coffee or lunch without having to make an extra call when you get back to the office.

Next on the list is **a pen**. If you find you are having a hard time remembering where you met people or what you promised them, jotting down a quick note on the back of their card can help. Of course, if you are going to do it in front of them, it's polite to ask permission. I haven't run into anyone who minds, but they appreciate that little extra show of respect. What's more, be aware in some cultures it's considered an insult to mistreat a business card — almost as if the card were an extension of the person.

Don't forget **your notebook**. You never know when you are going to want to take more notes than will fit on the back of a business card. It's distinctly possible that the card might be a dark color making your notes hard to read or it will be made out of indestructible space-age polymer. Nothing short of a welding torch will make a mark on it.

Oh, don't forget, networking events often include a presentation, which may contain an idea or two that you want to record. Coming from the world of the professional speaker, I love seeing someone taking notes during my presentation.

PREPARING EFFECTIVE TOOLS FOR BUILDING POWERFUL CONNECTIONS

Fourth on the list is... **business cards**. Business cards are still important, though not for the reasons most people think. For now understand that your networking success has nothing to do with the number of cards you hand out. Most people won't bother following up with you. If that's the case, you might ask, then why should you bother bringing your cards at all?

Actually, business cards have several good purposes. The first is simply that it **establishes credibility.** I'm sure you've experienced this. You are chatting with someone who claims to be someone really cool, like an international chef, or a race car driver, or a rocket surgeon. Fascinating, right? Then when you ask them for their business card, they don't have one. Doesn't it kind of make you doubt them just a little bit? In the world of networking, having a business card is the cover charge for being taken seriously.

Second, and this is probably the most important of the reasons: **Raffles.** Your card is your entry slip for every drawing at every vendor booth at the next trade expo you attend. Don't forget the local diner and the cupcake station. Winning a dozen cupcakes for the office is huge. It's even better if you work alone!

Next, your business card can be **a point of conversation**. I've had people, upon seeing my business card, comment on my logo or my title ("Superhero-in-Residence"). By the way, depending on what you do, that title can be a lot of fun. I've received cards in the past with the titles "Pilot" (he didn't fly a plane), "Chief Evolution Officer," and "Employee of the Month."

Finally — and this really *is* the most important one — it doesn't happen often, but **every once in a great while you will run into truly amazing networkers**. When they ask you for your card they have full intention to follow through and connect you with resource or opportunity. Don't miss out on this rare chance for lack of a simple card that, at least as of this writing, you can get for the cost of shipping from several online print shops.

Do have your cards with you; just *don't* assume they are going to create a connection in and of themselves. You might want to squirrel away a few extras in your car or briefcase. If you only give them out when asked, you should rarely run out, but it's nice to have a backup supply, just in case.

Back to our toolkit. Next up? Your **business card holder.** I like using a card holder just because it makes it easier to separate my cards from those that I get from others. It doesn't have to be anything fancy. You could even use a large paper clip or a rubber band in a pinch. The whole purpose is to help you avoid that fumbling search for your cards when someone asks you for one. Remember, *less stress means more you.*

Just a couple more items. If you have a **permanent nametag** that you like to wear, be sure that you get it on the pile, too. Occasionally groups require you to use a specific badge, especially if you are helping to host the event. Don't be that guy who forgot his.

Last item — and I know this may sound silly — **your clothes.** I have been made late on more than one occasion because I was running around the house searching for a shoe that had wandered from its normal location. Once again, laying out your clothes the night before serves to keep you relaxed and focused when you arrive at the event.

There it is — the list of physical objects to include in your toolkit. Be sure to lay everything out the night before. Make that practice part of your networking success ritual that starts you out each day in the right frame of mind.

INFORMATION TOOLS

Now that you know what you need to *bring*, what you need to *know*? Specifically, we will cover the necessary event information. Mostly you want to know this material simply to remove stress from the process of attending. You can find it from a variety of sources — the event website, the person who invited you, and especially the event organizer — and it shouldn't take you too long to gather it.

So what do you need to know?

First, **date and time.** I know this might seem to be obvious, but go beyond the obvious. Do a lot of people tend to show up early to network before the official event? Do they stay late? If you only set aside the time specified in the advertised schedule, you might be missing out on the best networking.

Second, **location.** Another seemingly obvious one, but you should ask about any quirks with respect to the location. Is parking available at the venue or will you have to park down the street? Do you need money for parking? How long will it take you to get there? Might any construction along your route cause a delay? If you've ever been hunched over the steering wheel driving just a little faster than you should while you watch the dashboard clock inch toward the time you were supposed to show up, then you know why this one is vitally important.

Speaking of important information, how about knowing a little about **who will be attending?** Will they be in your target market or (even better) will they be able to connect you to your target market? How many will be attending? The answers to these questions will help you to determine in advance whether this is a good event for you in general.

Next, **dress code.** You will seldom feel like more of an outsider than if your outfit doesn't fit the culture of the group. Don't stress about this. If you are a newcomer they'll likely forgive any slight fashion faux pas you commit. As long as you're close to what everyone else is wearing, you'll be fine. What you don't want is to show up in shirt sleeves when everyone is wearing a jacket and tie. This is important for your comfort, but there's a little more to it than that. It's about first impressions.

PREPARING EFFECTIVE TOOLS FOR BUILDING POWERFUL CONNECTIONS

We've heard the statistics. Depending on whom you believe, you have between two seconds and a minute to make a good first impression. Or, more to the point, when you meet a new person, they will make a snap judgment about the kind of person you are within that same amount of time — good, bad, or indifferent. A lot of people think that's just unfair.

I disagree.

Oh, their first impression might not be an *accurate* representation of who you are, but it isn't *unfair*.

Unfair is when you play a game and someone doesn't tell you all the rules. In this case, you do know the rule: Everyone you meet will judge you immediately and make a decision about you in the first few seconds. There, now you can't claim that first impressions are unfair.

How are you going to make sure those first impressions match up with who you really are? Remember, your fashion is a part of your first impression. Be remarkable, not bizarre.

Next up in the information toolkit, find out **the agenda**. Knowing when events are going to happen can go a long way toward helping you feel more comfortable. This is especially true for those groups and events that follow specific schedules.

You'll want to find out about any **special activities** they plan to do. I attended a networking meeting as a guest one time where one participant was chosen at random to present a challenge to the group for a round of peer advising. In this case, I wasn't selected for that honor, but the fact that I was ready with an issue made me feel a lot less likely to be embarrassed for lack of preparation. In another situation, our local Chamber had a lunch-time networking program in which they had a version of "pass the mic" where each person would stand and introduce themselves. The trick was that you could only say your name, your company name and *ten* additional words about what you do. Having to come up with those ten words off the top of the head probably added stress to more than a few people's lives.

We'll talk more about these activities and how to make them work for you in Chapter 9.

Related to the special activities, **do you need any materials** above and beyond what you would normally carry? I don't usually bring a lot of business cards with me (since I only give them out to people who ask — rarely more than four or five at a given event). Unfortunately, one event I attended expected you to pass a stack of cards around the table, so each person could take one. Fortunately for me, one of the organizers had a sheet of blank cards I could fill out to make up for the few I had with me. Unfortunately, that meant I wasted a lot of time that would have been better spent connecting with the other attendees.

Last but certainly not least, does the group have **any particular taboos**? I know groups that don't allow you to pass your card during their meetings. Others don't permit a guest to sign in without an accompanying member. While most attendees will forgive you for overstepping the rules when you are new, you'll still end up tarnishing that good first impression you were hoping to make. Better to know the boundaries and stay within them.

Remember, you want to feel comfortable at the gathering — or at least as comfortable as you can be while walking into a room full of strangers. Getting the lay of the land before you walk in the door can go a long way toward easing any apprehensions you might otherwise experience.

MENTAL TOOLS

You are now prepared with the physical toolkit and the event information you need to succeed at networking. Lastly, consider assembling two more pieces so that you ready and raring to go.

PREPARING EFFECTIVE TOOLS FOR BUILDING POWERFUL CONNECTIONS

Goals

First up, and most important is setting a goal for the event.

Suppose you find yourself at the Chamber of Commerce networking lunch. As you walk in, you see a number of people you know and several more who look to be new to this event. What do you do?

A. Go up and chat with the new people, or

B. Catch up with your old acquaintances

Think about it for a second. The answer, of course, is C — it depends. Either activity can benefit your networking. The trick is, before you even walked in the door you should have had a plan for your attendance at the event.

Personally, I usually want to meet the new people. Making connections with them is the way to expand my network. Still, chatting with old friends, at times, is more than just a pleasant pastime and can actually deepen the networking relationship.

Whichever way *you* choose, you should always have a goal and a reason for reaching it. Having a goal means you know when you've succeeded. It's hard to win a race when you don't know where the finish line is.

One aspect I am careful about though: I do try to make sure that any goals I set are almost completely dependent on my actions, not the actions of others. Anytime you try to break that rule, you're setting yourself up for a lot of frustration.

This is one of the reasons why trying to sell at the networking event isn't a good idea. Even if you set the goal of making only one sale, you are likely to walk away disappointed.

What *would* make a effective event goal?

For a new networker, I usually recommend the really simple approach: "Show up early. Find the buffet line, the coat room and the restroom. Say hello and introduce yourself to one person." For some of the folks I've worked with, this was the initial challenge they had to face.

If you're a little more advanced in your networking practice, depending on the event, setting a goal to introduce yourself to five people, or to have three five-minute conversations with people you don't know, or to offer to help the organizers set up for the event is more in order. You might focus on applying a new technique. Perhaps you'll ask four people what they like to do when they aren't selling widgets or find one benefit you gained from attending the event and then tell the organizer about it. Any of these would work as a specific event goal.

The other factor to consider is the format of the event itself. If you only have fifteen minutes to network and your goal is to have a conversation with ten different people, you're likely to miss that mark. At the same time, you want to challenge yourself, so saying you will introduce yourself to one new person when you are at a four-hour event might be letting yourself off the hook a little too easily.

Take a moment right now to think about the next event you are planning to attend. Taking into account the allotted networking time and your current skill level, what will be your goal? Just remember, in the end, you want to walk out of the event feeling like you really achieved worthwhile goals. The only way to do that is to know exactly what it is you are trying to do.

Homework

Next, you might consider preparing your homework. I know. You thought you'd left that behind when you left school. If it makes you feel more adventurous, let's call it reconnaissance.

If you've never attended this event before, who are the organizers? Not only what are their names, but what are their positions within the group? Look them up on LinkedIn to see if they have a profile picture. These folks are mega connected. Making contact with them is a huge advantage. Especially if you are new to the group, they will usually go out of their way to introduce you around.

Beyond the organizers, you might try to find out who else will be at the event. It's becoming less common, but a few organizers will still send out a list of people who've registered. Take a quick skim through it. Will you know anyone there? If so, great! Maybe you can agree to meet and do partner networking (see Chapter 10). Even if you don't know anyone, that's still fine. You can look for the folks you want to meet and verify that the other attendees are either in your target market or are a Success Connector for you.

If a speaker is scheduled to be at the event, find out more about them. What will they be presenting? What is their level of expertise? What are good questions you might ask? Take a few minutes to do the following:

1. Do a Google search on them. If they aren't famous, you might have to limit by geographical region.
2. If they have a blog, read a few recent posts.
3. Likewise, if they're on Twitter, read their most recent tweets.
4. If you can find a picture of them, glance at it so you will know them on sight.

The speaker is likely to be an outsider to the event. Doing just a few minutes of prep will help you make them feel appreciated. And that's a great beginning to what could be a great relationship.

The more prepared you are *for* the event, the more relaxed and genuine you can be *at* the event.

THE ANSWER TO THE MOST POPULAR QUESTION

Now comes what is possibly the most important preparation you can make. If you get this right, people will be lining up to buy from you. You'll be popular. Your fellow attendees will pull out their rolodexes on the spot to send you business. What's that crowning jewel of your networking event prep?

Developing your elevator pitch.

And in case you didn't pick up on it, yes, that was my tongue firmly planted in cheek.

Here's the scoop. The elevator pitch, the value proposition, the twenty-, thirty-, or sixty-second commercial. What do they all have in common?

They aren't good networking.

Think about it. If your goal in networking is to establish powerful connections and relationships with *other* people, then the traditional "pitch" just doesn't work. I can think of at least five reasons why

One, it's focused on sales. Even the name tells you that. You're giving them your "pitch"; you are describing your "value." You're making them listen to your "commercial"! Tell me the last time you established a strong, personal, mutually beneficial relationship with the person who interrupted your favorite television program to sell you a paper towel. No difference here except it's harder for your victim to change the channel.

Two, it's all about you. If you're talking about your stuff, you aren't finding out more about them. That means you aren't connecting.

Three, it's just not conversational. Imagine having a nice chat with the person sitting next to you at the alumni association lunch. As a part of the natural ebb and flow of the conversation, you ask them what they do. Suddenly they stop being a human being and deliver thirty seconds of their highly scripted value proposition. Talk about a conversation killer!

Fourth, it's fake and more than a little manipulative. Imagine you ask someone what they do for a living. Instead of telling you directly that he's a dentist, he says "I make children smile!" Yuck. Whenever I hear a response like this all I can think is, "What is this guy *selling*?" Listen, you know when someone is trying to manipulate you into asking more about their business. They can tell if you're doing that, too.

Finally, at the bottom of it all, they just don't care. Or at least they *won't* care about your business until they *do* care about you as a person. Really, the only good side about these techniques is they're short. You at least won't be in danger of boring the other person to tears.

SEVEN SECONDS TO SAY WHAT YOU DO

Remember what we talked about earlier? First impressions are completely fair and you should expect those you meet to be making snap judgements about you. What kind of a first impression do you think you are making when you drone on and on about yourself and your business?

Not a good one.

Develop a brief response to the "What do you do?" question. In my informal polling of my audiences I've found that, for most people, you've got between seven and ten seconds before they're bored listening to you talk about yourself and your business. Make it straightforward. Those "cute" responses just make you look evasive, deceptive, and manipulative. The best phrase you can say will include who you help and how you do it — simply and succinctly. All you want is for them to remember a general sense of what you do. For example, I might say, "I work with associations who want to develop strong networking skills within their membership so they have more loyalty and a better bottom line." If they just remember that I teach people about networking or even that I do business training, I consider it a win.

Beyond this brief explanation, just stop talking. If they want to know more, they can ask. Until and unless they do, you can refocus the discussion on them, their business, and their interests. Then you can connect with them as a human being and not as a company.

Because that's really the only way you can make great networking connections.

And they won't have that glazed look to their eyes. Bonus!

SPECIAL CASE: COMMERCIALS AT CLOSED NETWORKING EVENTS

All that said, there *is* one time when you should have your commercial ready. Occasionally networking events give you an opportunity to introduce yourself to the rest of the attendees. For many of these you don't have a great deal of time, so sticking with your seven-second description is probably your best plan. Depending on the event, though, you may need to extend your commercial to thirty seconds or even a minute. With that amount of time you really should develop and practice what you are going to say ahead of time. See Chapter 9 on Thirty-Second Commercials.

A QUICK LOOK BACK

That brings us to the end of Part 1. Looking back at what we've covered thus far, you should now be able to:

- Adopt a positive, productive mindset about your networking practice.
- Find the possible groups and events that will meet your ultimate needs.
- Evaluate those groups on a variety of factors to make sure they fit your lifestyle and requirements.

PREPARING EFFECTIVE TOOLS FOR BUILDING
POWERFUL CONNECTIONS

- Build your networking toolkit with the physical, mental, and informational resources you'll need to be comfortable and prepared.

Now that we've gotten you to the door, in Part 2 we'll take a look at what to expect *at* the event. We'll also cover the tactics and strategies that will help you make the best use of your time.

PART

2

PREPARING YOUR ROAD MAP TO EVENT SUCCESS

"True navigation begins in the human heart. It's the most important map of all."

~ Elizabeth Kapu'uwailani Lindsey

YOU AREN'T HERE TO HAVE FUN

(But You Might If You Know What To Do)

Do you remember the first time you drove in a strange city?

If you're anything like me, it was stressful. I'm thinking of my first attempt to navigate the streets of Ann Arbor. I knew where I was and I knew where I had to get to. The trick was dealing with all the little quirks and turns and surprises along the way. At the time a lot of one-way streets crisscrossed the town so the directions to get *to* your destination rarely matched the ones to get back home. For me it was a white-knuckler the entire time and I only did it when I absolutely had to. It certainly wasn't fun.

Here it is now almost thirty years after those first scary trips and I don't think twice about hopping in the car and heading downtown. I know the tricky spots. I know the best paths. Heck, I even know where the good parking areas are. While I still drive there for a specific reason, now I can have fun while I do it — listening to the radio, talking with a passenger, or singing at the top of my lungs.

For many people, networking is a lot like driving in a strange city. They know where they are and what they want to achieve. It's all the fiddly bits in between that make it stressful and no fun. Just like driving, though, with a little experience, you can end up having fun while you achieve your ultimate goals.

IN THIS SECTION YOU'RE GOING TO:

- Pick up tools and tactics to make you more relaxed, efficient, and effective while you are at the event.

- Get a crash course on what to expect when you show up at the gathering.

- Learn about the common types of events and how to navigate them.

- Get a timeline for what you should be doing and when.

- Discover the secret strategies for dealing with the networking games and activities you might encounter.

- Learn how to network with a partner.

I know you have a specific reason for being at this gathering. You worked on it in Part 1. You aren't at the event to have fun, but you know what? You might just enjoy yourself in the process if you know what to do.

Check the rearview mirror, make sure you're buckled in, and get out the GPS as we look at the one tactic that will reduce your stress by about 95.7%.

5

GET PAST THE "STRANGER DANGER"

"Standing as a witness in all things means being kind in all things, being the first to say hello, being the first to smile, being the first to make the stranger feel a part of things, being helpful, thinking of others' feelings, being inclusive."

~ Margaret D. Nadauld

At the beginning of many of my live programs I ask the audience to share their reasons why they feel uncomfortable at networking events. Shouts of "Rejection," "Don't know what to talk about," and "Don't want to be sold to" ring out. Don't get me wrong, those, and others, are all reasons for discomfort. The funny part is, the real reasons are so ingrained that we don't even know we suffer from them. It all comes down to a simple phrase.

GET PAST THE "STRANGER DANGER"

"Never talk to strangers"

Most of us learned this idea so long ago we don't even remember it. All we know is Mom didn't want us chatting up every person we met. We heard it often enough that it became a part of the internal rules by which we run our lives.

Did it keep us safe back then? Maybe. Now that we're adults, though, it's become an obstacle to our success. We walk into a networking opportunity, such as the Chamber of Commerce breakfast. What do we see?

Strangers.

And what's Mom doing in the back of our heads? Screaming "Never talk to strangers" over and over again. Do you think that might influence the way you approach your networking?

You know what, though? It's not Mom's fault. She learned it from her parents. They learned it from theirs, and so on, and so on. Really, we can look to the evolution of our culture from tribal societies to explain this mental block. We held outsiders in suspicion. They could be a danger to "us." You can see that theme interwoven throughout the history of almost any society in existence. In fact, some of our darkest passages throughout history have their basis in that fear and distrust of those who are different. Strangers make us uncomfortable.

Oh, and before you try to claim that you are highly evolved and don't feel this way, ask yourself when was the last time (without consciously thinking about it) you walked into a conference hall and sat down next to a complete stranger and struck up a conversation. Isn't it far more likely that you looked around, first, for someone you knew and, if no one presented themselves immediately, you found an empty table and started checking your email?

IN THIS SECTION YOU'LL...

- Develop a new way of thinking about "strangers."
- Create your "host" mentality.

A NEW WAY OF THINKING

The only way we can deal with this dilemma is, first, to acknowledge that we have this underlying recording playing in the back of our minds. Ignoring it won't make it stop. We'll still act on what Mom's voice is telling us. "Never talk to strangers! Never talk to strangers!"

Second, we need to find a way to get past this programming. Here's the bad news. Techniques won't make it stop. Oh, I can, and will, teach you techniques to help you strike up conversations with just about anyone, but if you can't get past your "Stranger Danger" mindset, you'll never have the chance to use them.

No, a mindset problem can only be "fixed" by another mindset — one we consciously adopt, one that comes to us almost as easily as fearing the stranger. What could that be?

Let me ask you this: Have you ever thrown a party? Maybe a small dinner gathering? Or perhaps a birthday party for a child? For the sake of this discussion, pretend you are hosting a gathering next Saturday. Imagine further that you've invited Sally, one of your closest friends, who is, of course, more than happy to attend. One small problem — her brother, Tom, is visiting from out of town. Would it be fine if he came along? She'd hate to leave him home alone. You agree and the date is set.

The night of the party arrives and your guests start trickling in. You hear a knock at the door and, opening it, you see an unfamiliar gentleman standing on your welcome mat. "Hi, I'm Tom. Sally's brother? She called to say she's running late at work and told me to meet her here."

Now comes the important question: Do you ignore Tom? Do you slam the door in his face? Do you call the police to escort him off the property? After all, he is technically a stranger.

Of course not!

In fact, not only do you invite him in, but you probably lavish extra attention on him, making him feel welcome. You introduce him around and check in with him periodically to make sure he's having a good time. After all, you are the host and he is your guest. Part of your personal responsibility is to make your guests comfortable and happy.

What if you took this mindset to the networking event?

What if, instead of walking through the doors as a small child, terrified of strangers, you walk into the room as the host of the gathering, determined to make your guests comfortable and happy? Would it change how you feel? Would it change how you behave?

Suddenly, instead of seeking out a "safe" place to stand — either with your friends or alone in the corner — it becomes your responsibility to check in with each attendee. You would always be on the lookout for those poor lost souls, sitting in the corner, waiting for someone to rescue them.

Wouldn't your conversation change, too? Hosts don't spend time talking about themselves. They take an interest in those around them. In fact, this ties in with one of the underlying Laws of Good Networking:

It's almost never about you. It's almost always about them.

Listen, I'm not saying that you have to actually be the person in charge of the program — though you gain many benefits by doing so. I'm just saying when you take on the host persona not only will you feel more confident at your next networking event, but you will also choose the behaviors that are going to make you more effective.

CHAPTER 6

SHOW UP EARLY

"I figured this was the easy stuff, and if we couldn't show up on time, looking right and acting right, we weren't going to be able to do anything else."

~ Bo Schembechler

Question: What kind of host would you be if you showed up late for your own party? Answer: Not a good one. Definitely one who will be off-balance the entire evening. One who will be apologizing to everyone and won't be prepared to make your guests as comfortable as possible. When you feel that way, it's hard not to fall back into the "Stranger Danger" mindset. You certainly don't feel like the host.

One of the biggest obstacles to adopting that "Host Mindset" is when you show up late. Even showing up on time and finding the room already filled with other attendees deep in conversation presents an obstacle. While it isn't impossible, it's certainly more difficult to strike up a conversation with people who are already in groups. Walking into a situation like this, you feel like an outsider.

Here's what you can do: Act like a responsible host would and show up before it all begins. Show up early.

It might seem like a minor point. It's not. Remember how your mom was always saying, "It's just as easy to be ten minutes early as ten minutes late"? She knew. Showing up just ten or fifteen minutes early not only can make you feel more like the host of the gathering, it has a variety of other benefits as well. I've come up with nine.

IN THIS SECTION YOU'LL...

Learn the benefits of showing up early including:

- Owning the room.
- Doubling your networking time.
- Freeing yourself of excess stuff.
- Scoping out the venue.
- Choosing your "sweet" spot.
- Meeting the organizer.
- Meeting other early people.
- Parking.
- Building your reputation.

OWNING THE ROOM

Have you ever watched how cats behave? One will jump on a chair or the couch and settle in for a nap. A second might approach and want to join the first. He has to ask permission. If he doesn't, he risks getting his nose swatted by the incumbent. The first one present owns the spot.

With cats and with humans, possession is nine-tenths of the law. In a strange way, if you are the first person at the event (or the first attendee at any rate) you own the venue. Those who arrive after you will, subconsciously, see you as being someone of authority — especially if you show your confidence and act upon it.

No, you aren't going to swat people on the nose. You are going to start acting like the host.

The other benefit of owning the room is that cliques haven't formed yet. You get to be the nexus of any new groups that form (if you want to). That gives you a little bit more power and control of the networking environment. And that will only serve to make you more relaxed and better able to connect with those around you.

DOUBLING YOUR NETWORKING TIME

Depending on the type of event, by showing up early you can almost *double* your networking time. If you are of a mathematical bent as I am, your brain is seizing up right now trying to figure out how showing up ten or fifteen minutes early to an event is going to double your networking time. I mean, really, don't these proceedings go on for an hour or two?

Yes, it is true that most events run for an hour and a half to two hours. That time isn't all devoted to networking, though. It usually includes a meal and possibly another form of activity such as a speaker. Throw in the time it takes to register and find your seat, and your effective networking time can be as short as fifteen minutes — not a lot of time to complete that ambitious goal you picked before you walked through the doors.

That extra ten to fifteen minutes you gain from showing up early gives you a better chance of reaching your networking goals. The more goals you reach, the better long-term results you will see.

FREE YOURSELF

I travel all over the country speaking at conferences and training company staff on the importance of networking. When I return from one of these programs, sometimes after weeks, I'll often walk through the door to shouts of glee from my daughters, Kaylie and Abigail. They run pell-mell to me, demanding hugs and kisses. It's the best!

The only problem is, I often have my arms full with a suitcase and carry-on bag, which really limit my huggability quotient. In fact, I've now learned to ditch my accoutrements as quickly as possible — before my darlings hurl themselves upon me, preferably.

It's all about freeing yourself.

Similarly, when you first show up at a business gathering, you really aren't prepared to network. You might have your purse or briefcase, maybe a coat or an umbrella. Business people always seem to carry a lot of *stuff* with them. Even if you walk into the event on time, you still have to get rid of all of that stuff just to have a hand free to reach out to the other attendees. Arriving early allows you the opportunity to drop off all your gear, maybe check your coat (or at least drape it over the back of your chair), and check to make sure all of your materials are in place.

You can get rid of everything except those tools you need to succeed in your networking.

SCOPE OUT THE VENUE

My buddy Tim spent a summer on a road trip to nowhere in particular. He would pick a direction to drive. When it got toward evening, he would find a campsite and set up his tent. He spent two months doing this and loved the new perspectives it gave him.

Me? The lack of a specific destination would have driven me right up the wall.

Even in his wayward travels, though, Tim carried a map. When on the road, it's good to have an idea of what is available.

When you arrive early at the networking event, take the time to scope out the location. Find the buffet line, the dessert table, the beverage stand (especially the coffee!). Look for the coat room if one is available and by all means locate the restrooms. Knowing where all of the facilities are will not only make you more comfortable, but, again, others will see you as an authority (after all what kind of host can't point you toward the restroom?), and you just might end up being their hero.

CHOOSE YOUR "SWEET" SPOT

Has this ever happened to you? You show up at a lunchtime event. You are really looking forward to hearing the speaker. As you walk through the door, people are already getting their meals and grabbing seats. You see what appears to be a good spot. You drop off your coat and go grab your lunch. By the time you get back to your table, the organizer is introducing the speaker. As you sit down, though, you realize that in your hurry you've selected a chair with a pillar between you and the stage. It's good you were looking forward to *hearing* the speaker, because you certainly won't be seeing him!

Getting a good seat can mean different tactics depending on the situation and the person. My eyesight and hearing aren't what they were twenty years ago, so I usually like to find a spot near the front of the room. If you know you have to leave early, you might try to grab a seat near the door. Even if this particular event is a pure "mixer" event like a cocktail reception with no assigned seating, you might still want to scope out a position where you can keep an eye on the main entrance and/or the buffet line.

The other activities of the event might have bearing on the optimal spot. Here's where that event information you researched will come in handy. For example, if the room is full of round tables and you know that you will be standing and introducing yourself to your fellow attendees, sitting at a table in the center of the room probably won't be as productive as sitting toward the edge. In the center, at least half of the audience will always be behind you, no matter which way you turn. An edge seat means when you stand up to address the room, the audience is all in front of you.

MEET THE ORGANIZERS

You're at the networking event and you have the lay of the land. You are ready to network. With whom can you connect before the participants arrive? Think about it for a second. Before the first attendee, before the sponsors, even before the speaker, the first persons will be the organizers. These are the folks who are actually throwing the party. You may even have spoken with them when you called to find out more information about the event during your preparations. Do you think they might be well connected? You bet! Do you think it would be a good idea to get to know them? Again, yes!

Here's the trick. These folks are usually busy and possibly more than a little stressed with all the preparations. Stopping them for a friendly chat at this point isn't likely to endear you to them. No, the best way to connect with an organizer shortly before the event is with four little words. **"How. Can. I. Help?"**

At this point, they will respond in one of two ways. One, they will say "No, thank you." or, two, they will take you up on it.

If they turn you down, don't push. You will get credit for the offer. You will stand out as someone who was willing to make an effort for the group. When you next approach one of the organizers, during a calmer portion of the gathering, he or she will remember you and be more willing to connect and help you.

If they take you up on the offer, even better. Most likely it will be a relatively low-effort task, such as placing handouts at each seat. For the expenditure of a little time and energy they now see you as someone who has actually worked to support the group — making you more worthy of their assistance in the long run.

To be clear, though, I will repeat: Just make the offer and, if they say "no," move on. Many organizers already have a plan and your diving in to help without being asked may end up making more work for them. Being an irritant is not a good way to kick off a relationship.

MEET THE OTHER EARLY PEOPLE

The organizers are only one group of people who show up early. You have an excellent opportunity to meet the other folks who tend to show up before the event officially starts.

- **The Speaker:** Depending on the presenter, they are likely to be well connected. Professional speakers and experts who deliver programs as a part of their business tend to call upon their connections to find more opportunities. If they are successful, they probably have a fairly robust network. Of course, you can try to connect with them after the program, but that's when you'll have to share them with the rest of the attendees. Especially if you've done a little homework on their expertise, you can have a great conversation with them before anyone else starts lining up to chat with them.

  One caveat: Be aware that some speakers don't like to be disturbed before they go on, so do be respectful of their process.

- **Master Networkers:** These folks tend to show up early (for all the reasons we've been talking about). They tend to have a lot of influence with the group and know almost everyone

— and most will know them. Not only are they good to know for their networks, but they are quite comfortable making conversation, so if you aren't at ease making small talk, they can make it easier to slip into that mode.

- **Newbies:** One other group to be aware of is the newbies. These are the folks who show up early because they're afraid they might be late. Remember, just because someone is new to the group doesn't mean they aren't worth knowing. That poor lost soul standing off to the side, waiting for someone to talk with might actually be the CEO of his company. Be his hero and rescue him. You'll never know where it might lead unless you make the effort.

PARKING

Have you ever done this? You are driving to a new location. You type the address into your GPS and it informs you that it will take fourteen minutes to get there. You need to arrive by 3 p.m., so you leave at 2:45 — that extra minute will make all the difference.

Can you see where this plan is about to go wrong?

You arrive at the office complex right on time — and then spend the next five minutes trying to figure out where you are supposed to park. Then you have to walk from the parking lot to the building and the search within the building to find the correct room. You just went from on-time to ten minutes late.

I know this sounds like an extreme case, but once again it points to the importance of showing up early so that you will be more relaxed and feel less rushed. On a simpler level, the later you arrive, the further away you will park. It just stands to reason. Merely arriving on time might mean just a few extra minutes of walking — or running — across the parking lot.

On the other hand, you might encounter a more complicated situation. I attended a two-hour event in a nearby city a few years ago. I'd been to the location several times and I knew where to park. Unfortunately, unbeknownst to me, since the last time I had visited, the city had turned all of the city lots into one-hour parking. If I had only arrived on time, I wouldn't have been able to contact the organizer to find out where alternate parking facilities might be.

BUILD YOUR REPUTATION

I saved the best for last. This is the number one reason to show up early to any networking opportunity: To build your reputation.

Someone who arrives early projects the image of being organized, focused, and serious about building their business. They give the impression that, for them, time commitments are sacrosanct and deadlines are more than mere suggestions.

When I see someone consistently showing up prepared before the door opens, I know that is someone who will take any referral from me seriously and treat the person I refer like royalty.

On the other hand, I have to wonder whether someone who is perpetually late will show that same lack of attention to those I might refer — which means I'll probably send those referrals to someone else. Showing up a little early and being prepared may seem like a little detail, but, as the late UCLA Bruins basketball coach John Wooden said, "It's the little details that are vital. Little things make big things happen."

So those are the nine reasons to show up early. To tell you the truth, I can't think of a single good reason for being late. Can you? Remember another of Mom's little sayings the next time you are figuring out when to leave for the meeting.

"Early is on time. On time is late."

7

WHAT TO DO WHEN: A NETWORKING EVENT TIMELINE

"How did it get so late so soon? It's night before its afternoon. December is here before it's June. My goodness how the time has flewn. How did it get so late so soon?"

~ *Dr. Seuss*

As long as we're talking about being timely, let's delve in a little deeper and come up with a timeline for attending the event. What happens during the event is dependent on what type of gathering it is. What happens before and after the event, however, is similar no matter what kind of event it is. For right now we'll focus on the details before and after. Knowing what to do and when can make you more relaxed and confident that you are being as efficient as possible with the whole process.

IN THIS SECTION YOU'LL...

- Learn the series of activities to pursue to be successful at the event.

- Discover what you should be doing after the event has ended.

BEFORE EVERYTHING

We've already talked about this in detail, but it bears repetition. **Before everything else, make sure you know why you're attending this event in particular.** Will the other attendees be in your target market or will they be Success Connectors who can *refer* you to that target market? Maybe you are primarily going for the content, or perhaps you just want to check out the event to see if it's one you should consider attending on a regular basis. Whatever it is, make sure you have a reason for showing up.

UP TO ONE WEEK BEFORE

For the period up to about a week prior to the event, do the following: **First, pre-register. Second, if you are so inclined, invite a guest.**

Pre-registration will get you the following benefits:

- **It can often mean a reduction in price.** Look for that early-bird registration discount whenever you can and be sure to take advantage of it.

- **Those who pre-register often get pre-printed name badges** — usually nicer and easier to read than the handwritten ones.

- **Most importantly, it's just nice to do.** It makes the organizer's life a little easier and, assuming you attend regularly, it's likely to make your name stand out to them.

As far as inviting a guest goes, we'll talk more about partner networking in Chapter 10. For now, just know that **inviting someone to an event is good networking practice**. Think about it. By offering to bring a guest, you are saying that you value that person's success. That person is likely to reciprocate.

ONE WEEK BEFORE

Moving on, one week before, **contact the event organizers**. Do you remember all of that event information we talked about in part one? The information about the venue, the agenda, and the dress code? At this stage, find that out these types of details. Of course, if you've been to this particular event before, you might not need to go into great depth, but you could ask if anything out of the ordinary would occur at the meeting or if you could help with a task. If I'm new to the event, I will actually give a call. For those where I'm already familiar with the proceedings I might just go with a quick email message.

Take a few minutes to do this. In addition to the information you receive, it's another opportunity to connect with the organizers.

THE DAY BEFORE

The day before the event, **confirm with your guests**. Make sure you share your event information with them. Especially if you are a long-term member of the group, you want to be known as someone who brings in new potential members. The best way to increase those chances is to make sure any guests you invite are at ease and ready for whatever the agenda might throw at them. You should discuss your **partnering strategy** (see Chapter 10).

In addition, this is a good time to do your research on the speaker or presenter, if one has been scheduled. You don't have to be ready to write their biography, but you could know enough to ask a good question or two. A quick Google search should be sufficient to get you that information.

THE NIGHT BEFORE

On the night before the event, take a few moments to **set out your networking toolkit**. Make sure you have all the physical items, of course, but double check all the informational ones, too. In addition to knowing where and when the event will be and how long it will take to get there, you might want to do a quick check on the weather or even the expected traffic levels for that time of day. You don't want any surprises that might delay your arrival.

On your list of preparations should be to **set your specific goals for the event**. Make sure you are aware of the amount of networking time you'll have so you can set those goals to be challenging, but not impossible.

BEFORE SET OUT

On the day of the event, set up your schedule so you leave with enough time to walk through the doors at least ten to fifteen minutes early. As we discussed in the last chapter, arriving early is by far the most powerful tactic you can employ to be more effective at the event.

IN THE CAR

While traveling to your destination, **review your goals**, but also do whatever you can to **focus your mindset**. Remember you do not want to be sales-focused (whatever "sales" might mean to you). Rather you want to focus on the idea of connecting with the people you meet — forming relationships.

It might sound easy, but we all have that devil on our shoulder who whispers temptations in our ear. Most of the time, he's easy to ignore, but he's less so when he's telling you, "Hey, you have a mortgage to pay and children to feed. You only talk with people who might buy from you. Save that relationship stuff for another day." It begins to sound like a good idea. Instead, listen to the angels of your better nature and know that establishing relationships *first* will lead to a greater payoff in the long run.

TEN TO FIFTEEN MINUTES BEFORE

You've arrived at the venue. **Do a quick self-inspection.** Make sure everything is in place. Maybe pop a quick breath mint. Straighten your shoulders and head in the doors. As soon as you can, **check in at the registration desk,** then **find a seat and drop off all of your stuff.** Next, **find the organizer,** introduce yourself, and offer to help set up.

From this point until the end, the type of event will define the specifics of what you should be doing. We'll be diving into that in a few minutes. Let's jump now to the end of the event and talk about what happens next.

FROM THE END UNTIL FIFTEEN MINUTES AFTER

This is your last chance to get in a little networking. You should **finish up that networking goal** if you haven't done so already. In addition, if you didn't already set up meetings for coffee or lunch with the people you met, now is a good time to catch them before they head out the door. Scheduling now will be a lot easier than trying to schedule later. Take time to **thank the speaker and the event organizers** if possible. Did you acquire an idea that was particularly meaningful? Now would be a good time to let them know.

BY THE END OF THE DAY

Enter all business cards into your card processing system, whatever that might be. If you don't, I can guarantee such a large amount time will elapse that by the time you *do* actually process the cards, you won't have a clue who these people are. This is especially true for all people with whom you were unable to set up a future meeting.

WITHIN TWO OR THREE DAYS

Actually **make contact with these people.** If you don't, then attending the event in the first place was to some extent, wasted. Your main reason for attending events is to meet new people. Meeting them is only the beginning, though. To make it worthwhile, you have to continue the association.

BEFORE TWO OR THREE WEEKS HAS PASSED

Meet them for coffee or lunch. Think of that get-together as an audition. After that meeting, you have to make the decision whether to add them to your long-term network.

QUESTIONS YOU SHOULD ASK YOURSELF:

1. **Did you have good chemistry with them?** If you are not connecting on a personal level, then you won't want to devote time and effort to helping them out.

2. **Do they seem to be good networkers?** The strength of your network is not in the number of people you know, but rather in the number of people they know.

3. **Are they even interested in maintaining a long-term networking relationship?** For whatever reason, right now might not be a good time for them to build their network. Maybe their business is currently inundated, or maybe they are going through family drama. Whatever the reason, respect their needs and maybe someday it will turn around.

> **4. Can you develop this relationship so that it's mutually beneficial?** The big question is whether or not you are able and willing to help them. You do *not* want to be the person who is only taking from the relationship. We've got names for people like that and none of them are complimentary.

This first meeting is all about whether it makes sense to put forth your precious time and energy into extending and strengthening the connection. If yes, great! If not, don't worry about it. Sometimes two perfectly wonderful people just don't mesh, for whatever reason. You are a serious networker and you know that you will be meeting new people all the time, some of whom will actually be good fits as long-term referral relationships, so don't get hung up on the ones that aren't quite right.

That's the general timeline of what you should be doing before and after the event. The "before" is focused on making you at ease. The "after" centers on making you productive and (eventually) profitable.

Obviously, you may have timelines for different events going on at the same time. You might be preparing to attend the Chamber lunch next week while you are following up on the Trade Association annual conference you attended last week. Don't think you have to be completely done with one gathering before you consider attending another.

Now we move onto the gap we left in the middle — what to expect when you are actually at the event.

CHAPTER

8

FIVE TYPES OF NETWORKING EVENTS AND HOW TO MAKE THE MOST OF EACH

"This is the power of gathering: it inspires us, delightfully, to be more hopeful, more joyful, more thoughtful: in a word, more alive."

~ Alice Waters

Here's a shocker. Are you ready? Not all networking events are created equal. I know. I know. I'll give you a second to recover from that revelation.

Every event has its own personality. The organizers, the activities, and, of course, the attendees give each a culture that is as unique as a fingerprint. That said, the *structure* of a particular gathering does fall into general categories. We can use that knowledge to prepare to get the most out of any given event, even if we've never attended it before.

Let's explore the different types and what tactics to use in each case.

FIVE TYPES OF NETWORKING EVENTS AND HOW TO MAKE THE MOST OF EACH

IN THIS SECTION YOU'LL...

- Learn how to get the most out of the Mixer.
- Master the variations on the basic Mixer (e.g., Activity, Meal, Trade show).
- Prepare yourself to be a guest for the Leads Passing Event.

MIXER

Using an automobile motif, first up is the base model, the Mixer. Almost all of the other types of events share aspects of the mixer and so the techniques that work splendidly here will apply to those other categories as well.

What is a mixer?

Effectively it's **a bunch of people gathering in one place and sharing polite conversation**. While you will hear a brief announcement or two, in general, no specific central agenda items, such as a speaker or a meal, takes place. The organizers *may* include icebreaker activities, but the primary goal is to bring people together so they can connect with each other. While a meal is not served, it's entirely possible that refreshments will include finger food, soft drinks, and (depending on the event) even alcohol.

In addition to "mixers," we might refer to these as "cocktails," "meet and greets," or "receptions." The agenda is simple. Usually registration opens about fifteen minutes prior to the announced start time. Then the event starts and people talk and mingle until they leave. Mixers can last from one to four hours with most in the two-hour range. Typically, organizations will *not* put on a standalone mixer. They've found that people won't show up for pure networking. As a result, most mixers you attend will be part of the larger event such as a conference or annual convention.

The problem most people have with these networking

opportunities is the unstructured nature of the event. They don't have a good framework for their networking. As a result they wander around lost or latch on to the first person they know and not let them go for the rest of the time.

What's the best way to deal with this beast?

First, and this applies to all of the remaining types so I'll only say it this one time, **do all the preparation we talked about in Part 1**. In particular, you must know what your goal is for the time you'll be attending. This will help protect you from the natural tendency to stick with the people you know the entire time (unless that happens to be your goal). It will allow you to know when you are done and can leave. Especially for the longer events, advanced preparation can save you from spending more time than you need away from your home or office.

Second, **whatever your goal is, adapt it if possible to a venue where small talk is the order of the day.** Mixing and mingling is what you are supposed to be doing. Conversations should usually cover five to ten minutes, rarely longer. It's difficult to have deep communication without being interrupted regularly. Don't try to fight it. The Mixer is perfectly suited to meeting new people and learning a little bit about them. Then, if it makes sense, exchange contact information or schedule a follow-up meeting.

We'll cover specific conversational techniques in Part 3, but for now just know that if you aren't actively chatting with someone or seeking out a new person to connect with, you probably won't be successful at the Mixer.

Advantages:

1. You have opportunities to meet many people.
2. The atmosphere is relaxed and social.
3. You can easily control the amount of time you spend at the event due to its relatively unstructured nature.

Disadvantages:

1. Conversations won't be particularly deep.
2. Lack of structure means you have to be disciplined yourself.

Tactics:

1. Set specific goals for what you want to accomplish.
2. Make sure those goals are appropriate for the length of time you have available to you.

SPEAKER/ACTIVITY

Sometimes the mixer base model has an option or two. More plainly, the organizers might have included a speaker or another central activity in the event's agenda. Call them seminars, workshops, or panel discussions; the primary reason for the event is no longer only connecting with other people. Now you have this other feature that will draw people to attend.

This can work to your advantage.

Most people who avoid networking events like they would a root canal might still show up for an Activity Event. They may be fans of the speaker or just have a real interest in the topic at hand. If the subject of the event might be of particular interest to your target market, then you've got a better chance of connecting with that group.

How do you make it pay off?

First, take a look at the agenda. In general, as with the mixer, registration will start about fifteen minutes prior to the formal beginning of the event. From that point until the main activity actually starts is a period of what they call "open networking." Guess what this is? Yep! It's a Mixer!

At this point, you can just follow the same techniques we've already discussed to connect with the other attendees. The only

FIVE TYPES OF NETWORKING EVENTS AND HOW TO MAKE THE MOST OF EACH

difference between "open networking" and a true Mixer is usually duration. Most Activity Events only devote between fifteen and forty-five minutes to networking — rarely as long as an hour. This means you need to be on task with your goals. Ideally you should complete those goals by the time the organizer calls the gathering to order. To be successful, you may need to adjust that goal to be realistically possible within the time allotted.

After the activity ends, usually people will hang around for an additional fifteen minutes or so, but you can't count on that. For most, the end of the show is the end of the event and they are heading for the garage, therefore don't count on being able to do more than connect with one additional person.

What should you do in between?

As a speaker myself, I know a lot of people view me as the "floor show" or "dinner theater." I'm to entertain and educate, but, as far as they are concerned, paying attention to me is about as necessary as paying attention to the background music in the elevator. It could be interesting, but if you have better tasks to do, then you should do them, right? This is why, when the speaker starts talking, you'll often see people pulling out their smart phones and checking Facebook, their email, or those cute little figurines they bid for on eBay.

Don't do it. It's bad networking.

Three big networking reasons to keep your focus on the person at the front of the room are:

1. **Discussion.** Paying attention will give you topics to talk about with the other attendees and also with those you might meet later who didn't get to attend the event.

2. **Connection.** As a professional speaker, I can tell you if you come up to me after I speak and tell me about a specific piece of my presentation that either really spoke to you or that you will use to make your life better, I will love you forever.

FIVE TYPES OF NETWORKING EVENTS AND HOW TO MAKE THE MOST OF EACH

Despite appearances, speakers are a bundle of insecurities just like everyone else. They appreciate knowing that their efforts haven't been wasted.

3. **Reputation.** As an audience member, when I see someone near me checking the results of their fantasy football league during a presentation, that person goes down a notch in my eyes. Their inattention tells me they don't value improving themselves and that they probably don't have the ability to focus on a situation for longer than a few minutes. Probably not someone I want to refer if I can avoid it.

True, sometimes you really do need to check on news back at home or the office. Be honest, though, those occasions are few and far between. You have to ask yourself whether the message that *might* be waiting is really worth alienating the people you are with right now. Most of the time, unless it is truly a matter of life and death, it isn't.

It can wait for twenty minutes.

Advantages:

1. Central activity, especially if it is a speaker/presenter, brings out "non-networkers."
2. Information from speakers can provide resources that you can pass along to your network.
3. Structure helps focus the networking effort.

Disadvantages:

1. The activity reduces the time available for making new connections.
2. Socially more difficult to sneak out when the program has started.

FIVE TYPES OF NETWORKING EVENTS AND HOW TO MAKE THE MOST OF EACH

Tactics:

1. Be aware of the agenda ahead of time. How much time is allotted for networking?
2. Set specific goals appropriate for the length of time you have available to you.
3. If members of your target market would be interested in the topic, invite them to attend.

MEAL

Probably the next most common category is the Meal Event. Breakfast, lunch, dinner, High Tea, or midnight snack, it seems like mealtime and networking go hand in hand. Usually, though, it's not just a matter of coming through the door, grabbing your food, and plunking down in the nearest unoccupied seat. Or at least it shouldn't be.

Again, registration usually starts about fifteen minutes before the formal beginning time. Then, as with the Activity Event, you'll usually have a period of open networking. After that, the meal starts and you either go through the buffet line or have wait staff serve you at the table (which is usually the sign of a more formal shindig). Often a speaker presents or another central activity occurs; then, after the dishes are cleared and the presentation is over, you'll have ten to fifteen minutes of "unofficial" open networking, again, similar to the Activity Event.

Why don't we just treat this as an Activity Event and be done with it? Actually, despite many similarities, one significant difference exists. The Meal Event has three different styles of networking. Each has its own advantages, but you have to approach each in its own way.

FIVE TYPES OF NETWORKING EVENTS AND HOW TO MAKE THE MOST OF EACH

MIXER

We've already talked about how to deal with this. As with the Activity Event, you still have a limited time and now you have one more constraint. Ideally, during this time, you might want to scope out potential table mates. Why? Because of the second type of networking — seated or stationary networking.

STATIONARY NETWORKING

Mixer-style networking allows you to connect with many people with the trade-off that those connections tend to be relatively shallow. You don't have the ability to get into a deep conversation during the five or ten minutes you are chatting — especially when other participants are continually interrupting the flow of the conversation. Stationary networking, on the other hand, flips that. You can usually have a more significant interaction. The downside is you only get to connect with the people on either side of you. If you discover that one isn't someone you want to connect with at all, ever, you're kind of out of luck.

Unless seating is assigned, you should have a secondary goal of your mixer time — to keep an eye out for someone whom you'd like to get to know better during the stationary period.

BUFFET LINE

The third type of networking is the buffet line period. This is for those events where you actually have to go up and get your own food. For the most part, you want to minimize this portion of the networking. It has the disadvantages of stationary networking since you can really only chat with the people on either side of you and, because you are distracted by other matters like balancing your food, it also has the downside of mixer networking — relatively shallow connections. About the only benefit you get during this time is a shared activity, which can make starting conversations a little easier.

FIVE TYPES OF NETWORKING EVENTS AND HOW TO MAKE THE MOST OF EACH

Unless the person you really want to meet is just entering the line, let the initial rush of people getting food die down a little bit. You can take that time to chat with prospective lunch companions. Even if you are returning to the table alone, the people waiting on either side of you will probably have exhausted the conversation with their other seat mate and will look forward to seeing you.

Of course, pay attention to the presentation for the same reasons as we've already discussed for the Activity Event. After everything is done, you'll have a few minutes of post-event mixer style networking before everybody leaves.

Advantages:
1. Open networking period allows you to meet new people.
2. Stationary networking allows you to create a deeper connection with your seatmates.
3. Event structure focuses your networking effort.

Disadvantages:
1. The event structure reduces the time for making new connections.
2. Food can distract from the networking effort.
3. You can get trapped next to someone with whom you don't want to connect.

Tactics:
1. Add "Find good table companion" to your list of goals.
2. Be aware of the agenda ahead of time. How much time is allotted for networking?
3. Set specific goals appropriate for the length of time you have available to you.
4. Don't rush to the buffet line unless you want to stand next to someone in particular.

TRADE SHOW

The fourth event type has a mixture of the other types, plus a dash of its own style. This is the Trade Show Event.

This type goes by other names including "Annual convention," "Association conference," and "Business Expo." Essentially this is a longer event — from a half day to multiple days — with more people — hundreds or thousands — and often requires travel to attend. The nice characteristic of these events is they take away a lot of the time pressure you have in a smaller standard networking event. The downside is they can be completely overwhelming and you might end up wasting a lot of time if you don't go in with a strategy.

First understand that **these events are made up of smaller segments which mimic the other types.** Pull out the schedule for one and you'll find a continental breakfast is scheduled for 7:30 to 8:30. That's just a Meal Event. You might have an opening keynote presentation or a morning breakout session. Those are Activity Events. Perhaps they've scheduled a cocktail reception in the evening or they have a hospitality lounge open all day where you can go relax and enjoy light refreshments — Mixer Events!

When you set your goals, you can fine-tune them for the individual segments. Doing this is a lot more manageable than trying to set goals for the entire event. Of course, **if you are going to be attending an event like this one, you *must* take a look at the schedule in advance.** Plan out your itinerary for the time you will be at the event so you can maximize your networking opportunities.

How is this event different? First, **this is a marathon, not a sprint.** Cut back on your usual networking goals for any given time period or you'll burn yourself out and you won't have the energy to connect with the people you *do* meet. Leave a little time for quiet reflection — especially if you're an introvert like I am. A couple of years ago I

FIVE TYPES OF NETWORKING EVENTS AND HOW TO MAKE THE MOST OF EACH

went to the annual convention for the National Speakers Association. I had a fantastic time, learned a lot, and made great contacts. I also had to take time out about every two or three hours to find a quiet place where I could process all of the inputs from the day.

In fact, a corollary of this strategy is to examine all of the program offerings and prioritize them. Which must you absolutely, positively attend? Which ones should you skip because they have no real bearing on your life? Which ones would you *like* to attend, but would skip if you found yourself in a great conversation? The programming at these events can be educational, but often the best return on your investment will come from the conversations you have in the hall. Be ready to change your schedule, if necessary.

As long as we're talking about modifying your goals, **determine in advance the people with whom you want to connect**. Of course you want to meet **new people**. I would never frown on that strategy. If this is an annual event, like NSA's annual convention that I attended, and you are a regular participant, then you should be spending at least a part of your time re-connecting with **people you already know**. You might even schedule with them ahead of time to meet for dinner or an evening outing. Even if you already maintain contact with them over the year, being face-to-face goes a long way toward strengthening the relationship.

One other group to consider is **your coworkers and colleagues**. Many view an out-of-town event like this as a good opportunity to connect outside the office. Of course, you have to decide what combination of groups would be most advantageous for you, but having a good mix of starting new connections and strengthening old ones will give you the best return on your attendance.

The other big difference between a Trade Show Event and other types is the exhibition hall. Here vendors have paid to have booths to connect with you, their target market. If you aren't one of these vendors, then you can view the hall as a giant mixer. You can connect with fellow attendees, but also take the opportunity to reach out to vendors.

A couple of caveats here: First, the vendors have paid good money in the hopes of getting a return on that investment, which means that many of them will think they should be selling. Don't be too offended if they don't get around to asking you about you. Second, during the busiest of times, try not to monopolize their attention as they have a job to do.

The best vendors understand that this isn't really a sales moment, but a networking opportunity. If it's a relatively quiet time, they'll love to sit back and chat with you. Especially if you are new to the event, they can be a fountain of great information about what to see and do. Be interested in them, their products, and especially who their target market is. Maybe you or someone you know would like more information about the services they offer. You could make a friend for life!

As with any of the event types we've discussed, be sure to follow up afterward. You can't measure your success by the number of cards that you've exchanged, but rather by the number of connections you've started.

Advantages:

1. Extended duration removes many time constraints.
2. Variety of networking sub-segments allows you to work in venues where you have the most comfort.
3. Larger numbers of people increase opportunities.
4. You have opportunities to reconnect with those whom you already know.

Disadvantages:

1. Sheer scope of program can be overwhelming.
2. Cost in both time and money can be prohibitive.

FIVE TYPES OF NETWORKING EVENTS AND HOW TO MAKE THE MOST OF EACH

> **Tactics:**
> 1. Review schedule before the event to be strategic about your networking goals.
> 2. Reduce the scope of goals for any given segment in comparison to a similar event outside the Trade Show.
> 3. Be ready to modify your plans and goals as necessary.

LEADS PASSING

I've saved this last type for the end because it's kind of its own creature. This is the Leads Passing Event.

We discussed Referral and Leads Passing Groups back in Chapter 3. Here, I will explain specifically what to do when you are invited as a guest. Remember, each of these groups has its own rules, frequency of meetings, and specific agendas. Underlying them all, though, are two concepts: The purpose of the group is for members to provide referrals to each other and, usually, no more than one member from any given industry is in attendance.

Most of these groups have a secondary drive to invite guests — it's where new members come from — so don't be surprised to find yourself attending many of these meetings as a non-member. If one of your networking connections invites you to attend a meeting as their guest, be sure to ask her exactly what you need to prepare.

Members often gather before the formal start of the meeting for open networking. When the organizer (or president or facilitator) calls the program to order, you can expect a short period of general group business — often general announcements and sometimes a networking tip. Then a round of introductions takes place. First, each member stands and delivers a short thirty to sixty second "commercial" about his or her business. As a guest, you will also have the opportunity to introduce yourself, but usually after all of the members have gone. You'll want to be ready for that (see the section on thirty-second commercials in Chapter 9).

After the short introductions, one or two members will then deliver a longer "educational" presentation — usually lasting between five and ten minutes each. This allows them to talk about their business in greater depth and request specific actions from the rest of the group. As a guest you would never have to participate at this level. Simply sit back and learn about them.

After the longer presentations, each member in turn reports on any referrals he or she has for other members of the group. As a guest, your participation in this segment will again be reserved until the end. If you need someone's services, of course, let them know. If you don't, don't worry about it. They may, though, ask you to say a few words about what you experienced at the meeting.

Depending on the group, you should ask your host if any other specific preparations need to be made. Do you need to bring a pile of business cards? Probably a good idea to know about that.

As a guest, assuming your industry is not already represented by an existing member, expect a recruiting effort. Don't be surprised when they hand you a folder with information on how to become a member. Typically, you may attend as a guest for only a limited number of times before you are expected to make a decision on whether or not to join.

Advantages:

1. You meet people who are focused on networking to build their business.
2. Meeting usually won't cost anything to you as a guest (though your host/sponsor may have to pay).

Disadvantages:

1. Members of the group focus on passing referrals to other members. As a guest, because the other attendees don't know you yet, you won't receive any referrals yourself.
2. You only get a limited number of visits as a guest.

Tactics:

1. Prepare your introductory thirty- or sixty-second introduction before you walk in.
2. Be sure you know how much time is allotted for that introduction.
3. Connect with members during the open networking times and be sure to follow up.

Those are the five main types of networking events. You may experience others in your networking career, but most can be boiled down to fit one of these categories or a combination of them. Follow these strategies for success.

9 PLAY TO WIN: TWELVE GAMES AND ACTIVITIES AT THE EVENT

"Just play. Have fun. Enjoy the game."

~ Michael Jordan

Talking about the Leads Passing Event in the last chapter brings up the importance of having foreknowledge of what activities the event might hold. I hate being unpleasantly surprised by a "networking game" that I'm not prepared for. At the very least it puts me off balance. Worse, it can end up being a complete waste of time if I don't have a good strategy to make it pay off.

Event organizers try to come up with new ways all the time to help attendees have more fun — or at least be more effective — in their networking efforts. While not all of these are "games" per se, they do deviate from the normal mixer-style we've talked about. Are all of them effective?

PLAY TO WIN: TWELVE GAMES AND ACTIVITIES AT THE EVENT

As you might have guessed, some are, some are not. Many depend on who is doing the networking. I've broken them down into what I see as the good ones — the ones that promote and enhance the process of making connections — and the bad ones — the ones that dehumanize or encourage limited networking behavior. In this chapter, I'll navigate you through a few of them, what they are, and how best to prepare, if possible. At the end of each description is a brief summary of the advantages, disadvantages, and tactics for success.

IN THIS SECTION YOU'LL...

- Prepare yourself for one of the most popular activities — Speed Networking.
- Discover the tactics to succeed with other beneficial networking games.
- Learn the activities you should avoid.

THE GOOD

First up we have the activities I've encountered that actually help the networking process or at least don't hurt it. With these, be prepared with the right tactics and you will be able to make them pay off.

SPEED NETWORKING

One of the most popular networking activities is Speed Networking. Organizers create whole events with this as the centerpiece. We're going to spend more time on this activity than any of the others as it requires a little more skill to navigate successfully.

Speed Networking, as you might guess, is similar in concept to speed dating. You're usually seated at a long table facing another attendee. The actual amount of time can vary, but usually you've got between two and four minutes to get to know each other. At the end of that time one side of the table moves one seat to the left (or right) and you start the process again with a new person.

This activity has advantages because it gives you a chance to meet people who would otherwise associate only with their friends or not at all. The downside is the conversation is about as deep as a puddle. Consequently, it can be difficult to get to know a person well enough to know whether it will be worth your time to connect later.

Here are strategies to keep in mind:

1. **Avoid hemming and hawing and start the conversation.** You have only limited time. Even two minutes (your half of a four minute time limit) will *fly* by. Jump in and get going.

2. **Respect the other person's time.** If you are a good conversationalist, this might actually work against you. If you start chatting without a focus, you may run into the other person's time, which means that they won't have a chance to learn about *you*.

3. **Respect *everyone's* time.** When the bell or buzzer sounds, you *must* gracefully terminate your existing conversation (though perhaps with a promise to continue later) and move on to the next person. If you don't, it will cause each participant upstream of you to miss out on networking time with their next person.

4. **Have your questions ready.** You probably have time for three questions at most after the introductions. I recommend going with the following:

   1. *"What brings you here today?"* This question gets to the point about what they might be hoping to achieve. They probably want more business, but maybe they are looking for an employee or a job.

   2. *"If I'm talking with someone, how would I know they are someone I should send your way?"* This helps you learn how to meet the need from question **1** *and* tells them that

you care about their success. You may not be *ready* yet to pass them a juicy referral (after all you've only spoken for a minute!) but you can at least see if you share a target market which is a good quality in a networking partner.

3. *"What do you like to do when you **aren't** working in your business?"* This will tell you more about *who* they are. Remember that despite the short time limit, you want to start developing a relationship. You'll need to know more about them as a person in order to do that.

5. **Be prepared with your answers.** If you ask them a question, expect that they will ask you the same question in return. Be ready with your own answers to those questions we just discussed.

6. **Be succinct.** You must be able to describe what you do in about ten seconds or less. Make it interesting, make it memorable, but, above all, make it short.

7. **Have a pen and paper handy.** You will really stand out in the crowd if you take a few seconds to jot down what you learn from each person — especially if it means that you can help them out at a later date.

8. **Have fun!** You won't be able to make every connection into a long-term referral source, but if you can turn thirty short conversations into even two or three productive relationships, then the whole experience is worth it.

Advantages:

1. You'll meet many people in a short period of time.
2. You can interact with people you might not have met otherwise.
3. "Limited networkers" can't monopolize your time.

Disadvantages:

1. You have only a short time with each partner.
2. Conversations can't be very deep.
3. So many people in such a short period of time can make follow-up difficult and confusing.

Tactics:

1. Stay within the time limit.
2. Follow directions.
3. Prepare questions in advance.
4. Take notes.
5. Follow up afterward.

VARIATIONS ON SPEED NETWORKING

Knowing how popular this activity has become, don't be surprised if you encounter variations on this theme. Each one provides its own advantages and disadvantages. Certain events may even combine these variations, so be prepared to dance when necessary.

ROOM LAYOUT

Sometimes the room is laid out as one long table. The person on one end has to run to the other end when the seat change comes. At times the layout includes two or more long rows. With this configuration you might either run to the end of your own table or move to the end of the next table.

I've even seen two massive concentric rings. No given layout has any particular advantage. All you have to do is make sure you listen to the facilitator so that you know the pattern you are supposed to follow.

As a skilled networker, you may have to be prepared to jump into an empty seat should someone in front of you get confused and steal your seat. This isn't musical chairs. You will find another empty seat somewhere in the room.

By the way, if you are organizing an event like this, make floor signs or clear directions at any point where the participants might get lost or confused.

Advantages:

1. None.

Disadvantages:

1. Different layouts can cause confusion, which can lead to bottlenecks in switching partners.

Tactics:

1. Pay close attention to the organizer and help those around you if they get lost.

TABLE GREETINGS, FREE FORM

In this variation, you move from table to table, with each table holding six to ten people. Usually, each table grouping lasts about ten minutes. Often, a table host facilitates the activity. Each person gets a moment to tell the group about herself (see Pass the Microphone, below), and then a few minutes to answer questions from her tablemates.

The reason I call this "Free Form" is that you get to choose which table you go to next. To be successful, look for tables that have a high proportion of people with whom you've not yet had a chance to connect. Assuming you will have a chance to ask questions of each participant, be ready with your questions. There's nothing worse for some people than for them to screw up their courage to speak in front of a group only to be greeted by stony silence when the phrase "Any questions?" rings out.

Advantages:

1. You hear basic information about each person.
2. An entire table of people hears your information and may have questions.
3. Facilitator (if you have one) makes sure everyone has a turn.

Disadvantages:

1. Most people are nervous so they focused on what they are going to say and can't be interested in you.
2. Because it isn't a conversation, you can't make a real connection.

Tactics:

1. Prepare questions in advance.
2. Take notes.
3. Follow up afterward.

TABLE GREETINGS, FORMAL

Similar to the Free Form version of Table Greetings, you have a number of tables with six to ten people each. Often you will have a minute or so to introduce yourself to the group. The big difference here is someone has gone to the trouble to create a formalized series of tables you are to attend and that list is different for each person. The purpose of this version is to maximize the number of new connections you can make and to minimize your chances of finding yourself at a table full of people you've already met. Be aware of the table tags and follow your instructions and you will be fine.

I've seen variations of this version where the tables are grouped by shared traits. For example, all the people at the table might have the same or related target markets. What makes this version cool is that you know the rest of the people at the table will likely be good referral partners for you. The organizers went to the trouble of doing that research for you. Be sure to thank them!

Advantages:

1. You hear basics from each person.
2. Entire table hears your information and may have questions.
3. Facilitator (if you have one) makes sure everyone has a turn.
4. If system is designed well, you either are in front of many more people or a smaller group of people who are particularly well suited to be referral partners.

Disadvantages:

Same as Table Greetings, Free Form.

Tactics:

Same as Table Greetings, Free Form.

TABLE GREETINGS, ONE TO ONE

Again, this variation is performed at tables of six to ten. This time, in addition to everyone introducing themselves, you have the opportunity to speed network one-to-one with the person sitting next to you — sometimes both. Treat this opportunity as a Pass the Microphone (see below) and a Speed Networking. Be interested and then be conscious of the time. The big benefit of this variation is, by the time you talk with the person next to you, you should already know a little about what they do, so you should be able to get into a more substantive conversation.

Advantages:

1. You hear the basics from each person.

---

2. Entire table hears your information and may have questions.
3. Facilitator (if you have one) makes sure everyone has a turn.
4. Get to have a slightly deeper conversation with one or two people at each table.

Disadvantages:

1. Most people are still too focused on what they are going to say and so can't be interested in you.
2. The few conversations you have won't be particularly deep.

Tactics:

1. Prepare questions in advance.
2. Take notes. Pay particular attention during the self-introductions to those with whom you are likely to chat in the one-to-one portion of the activity. Knowing their basics will make the conversation deeper than might be possible during a short amount of time.
3. Follow up afterward.

PASS THE MICROPHONE

Enough about Speed Networking. The next activity is called "Pass the Microphone." Other names you might see are "Pass the Mic," or "Introductions." Many groups have this activity and it is that part of the agenda when each person gets to stand up and give a *very* brief description about himself. Certain events limit it by number of words, others by amount of time. While this activity isn't truly networking (really it's more marketing or advertising), it still helps people to get to know you a little bit. This process can be good if you are prepared. The challenge is to provide meaningful introductions in that short amount of time.

To that end, if you know that the event includes an activity like this, always, always, always prepare your statement ahead of time. Being boring isn't the worst outcome. What you really don't want to do is exceed whatever limit the organizer has specified. That is the unpardonable sin.

I remember attending networking lunches at the Ann Arbor Chamber of Commerce. They had a ten-*word* limit in addition to your name and company name. They even had sheets of paper to allow you to write down the ten words. If someone got up and launched into a long-winded description, you could almost *hear* the rest of the attendees rolling their eyes.

If you think about it, going beyond the limit is sending a bad message to the other attendees. By doing so, you are focusing more on yourself and your message than on being fair to the rest of the group. Not a good first impression when you are trying to create new relationships.

When it comes to the message, the usual topics you might include are a brief description of your business and maybe who you serve. If you are feeling particularly clever, feel free to have fun with it. Just (do I need to say it again?) *stay within the limit.*

Advantages:

1. You hear the basics from each person.
2. Entire room hears your information.
3. Emcee or host makes sure everyone has a turn.

Disadvantages:

1. The imposed limitations may be so constrained that you can't deliver a meaningful message.
2. Most people are too focused on what they are going to say and so can't be interested in you.
3. You aren't interacting, so no real connections made.

> **Tactics:**
>
> 1. Prepare whatever you are going to say in advance.
> 2. Stay within the limitations.
> 3. Watch for potential clients and referral partners.

THIRTY-SECOND COMMERCIAL

A longer version of Pass the Microphone is the Thirty-Second Commercial. Other names for this might be "Sixty-Second Commercial," "Member Minute," and "Partner Education." This version gives you the opportunity to talk for thirty to sixty seconds about yourself and your needs. You'll see this version almost always at Leads Passing Events, but it isn't necessarily exclusive to those venues.

Whenever you do this version you should start and end with your name and business. Speak clearly. Include what you do, who you serve, fascinating facts about your business or industry, maybe even a short story about what you've done recently, or any combination of these topics.

The one key element you must include is a call to action. Do you want to meet a particular person or be introduced to members of your target market? Do you need a particular subcontractor? Are you looking for resources to make your business run more smoothly? Tell them what you want. As with the Pass the Mic activity, unless you want to waste the opportunity, prepare and practice what you are going to say ahead of time. Winging it will lead to a less powerful presentation that either doesn't take advantage of the time available or ends up going over and getting cut off.

> **Advantages:**
>
> 1. You learn more about each person than merely their name and business.

2. Entire room hears your carefully crafted message.

3. Longer format allows you to convey more details, including how someone could help you.

Disadvantages:

1. Thirty to sixty seconds is still a very short amount of time.

2. Most people are too focused on what they are going to say and so can't be interested in you. Is it only me or do you see a pattern here?

3. You aren't interacting directly, one to one, with anyone so this is more marketing or advertising than relationship building.

Tactics:

1. Prepare whatever you are going to say in advance. Always include a call to action.

2. Stay within the limitations.

3. Watch for potential clients and referral partners.

4. Take notes.

5. Pay attention to any requests that you may be able to fulfill.

PARTNER INTRODUCTIONS

You'll see this one occasionally at all-day or multi-day seminars. One of the first activities the host will have you do is pair up and prepare an introduction about the person next to you. You do so and then, each in turn, stand up and present your partner to the rest of the group.

As uncomfortable as it can be to speak in front of a group, I do like this one. Think about it. You are basically required to find out information about the person next to you — a task that we should be doing at a networking event anyway. I recommend that you each take turns asking questions and, in fact, the organizer may have a list of questions for you to ask. You go first. Of course, ask the ones you are supposed to ask. Get through those quickly. Then start asking the good questions (the ones you want someone else to ask *you*). Your partner will likely mirror you and ask you the same questions in return. Not only that, they will then announce that information to the room at large! Be sure to ask questions like, "What is your target market?," "What are you hoping to get out of today?," and "What would be a good referral for you?"

Advantages:

1. You hear the basics from each person.
2. Entire room of people hears about you, your business, and what you want and it's coming from someone else. It isn't you bragging or begging.
3. You can control the conversation to make sure your partner delivers the information you want.
4. You start to develop a real connection with at least one person in the room.

Disadvantages:

1. Your partner may not pay close attention and provide wrong or even bad information about you.
2. Most people are too focused on what they are going to say and so can't be interested in you.

Tactics:

1. Have a set of questions to ask prepared in advance.
2. Write down your partner's information. That will prompt them to do the same.
3. Watch for potential clients and referral partners with other introductions.

ICEBREAKER QUESTIONS

As far as conversation starters go, Icebreaker Questions can be a nice addition to the gathering. When you're seated at the table, you might find a card or name tent with one or more "icebreaker" questions. These can be anything from the silly ("What was your favorite breakfast cereal as a kid?") to the sublime ("What book inspired you to become the person you are today?"). For anyone who has trouble starting the conversation, this isn't a bad way to get it going. In fact, sometimes it's the silly questions that help people find their common points of interest.

Even if you don't have an official list of icebreaker questions, you might bring in a few yourself, simply for the fun of it. I even use these in my voice mail message to humanize what could otherwise be a dehumanizing process. Here are a few of my favorites.

- What's your favorite movie?
- Where would you like to go on vacation?
- Who is your favorite superhero?
- What is your favorite flavor of ice cream?
- If you could choose anyone from history, living or dead, and have a conversation with them, who would it be?

Remember, this isn't an interrogation. The idea here is to have a little fun and get people to open up about themselves.

Advantages:

1. Questions give non-conversationalists topics to talk about.
2. Questions often focus on the personal, which is a better place to make professional connections.

Disadvantages:

1. Some people might think that the questions are silly or inappropriate to a business event and may choose not to play.

---

2. Could detract from existing conversations if someone at the table wants everyone to play.

Tactics:

1. Relax and have fun.
2. Pretend you are talking to a real, live human being. Be interested, curious, and fascinated.

ICEBREAKER WORKSHEET

In many ways, this activity is a close cousin to the Icebreaker Questions activity. In this one, usually done with groups of twenty to fifty, each person receives a copy of a worksheet that has a series of qualities on it. It might have phrases like "Owns a tuxedo," "Has visited Cuba," and "Comes from a large family."

The idea is to walk around the room and, without asking directly, find people who might fit into each category. This is usually followed by a facilitator walking around to each person in the room and asking what people know about him or her. Obviously, this activity can be time consuming and works best in kick-off meetings for long-term collaboration. I did it with a training group at the beginning of a year-long program where we met together once a month for a whole day.

The game itself may sound silly, but I love it. You get to find out strange and interesting facts about the other people at the event. At the program I mentioned I met someone who later became a close friend and advisor. She told me about her "visit" to Cuba, which wasn't so much a visit as it was their commercial aircraft accidentally flying into Cuban airspace and almost causing an international incident! That's the kind of information we learn about friends and personal connections and goes beyond merely creating a professional relationship for the purposes of doing business.

Advantages:

1. Questions give non-conversationalists a topic to talk about.
2. Questions often focus on the personal, which is a better place to make professional connections.
3. Appeals to the competitive player, forcing them to learn about others for "points."

Disadvantages:

1. People might think that the questions are silly or inappropriate to a business event and may choose not to play.
2. It's likely to be the primary purpose of the gathering given the time requirements.

Tactics:

1. Relax and have fun.
2. Be interested, curious, and fascinated. You will undoubtedly find out more about people as they will want to fit somewhere on the sheet.

RANDOM SEATING

Many years ago, I attended a breakfast networking event at our local Chamber of Commerce. I still wasn't particularly comfortable jumping into groups, but I was determined to make the effort. I got my plate of food and looked around for a likely table. There it was. All but one seat were already taken and the people were having a lively discussion. Perfect!

I approached and asked if the seat was taken. They welcomed me with friendly smiles. As I was getting settled, the gentleman on my right turned to me, "Bob Turner, from Big Local Bank" — by the way, the names have been changed to protect the guilty. The young woman on my other side held out her hand. "Meg Jones, Big Local Bank." I began to get a sinking feeling in my stomach as I scanned the rest of my table mates. Every single one of them was proudly sporting his or her "Big Local Bank" nametag. As I started eating my breakfast, they all returned to discussing business at that venerable institution — a conversation that definitely left me out in the cold.

Have you ever gone to an event, sat down at a table, and discovered that everyone else at the table worked at the same place? Doesn't really make for a productive networking meal; does it? Random seating isn't so much a game or activity as it is a particular technique that organizers can use to break up these groups who already know each other. One mechanism is to give each attendee a standard playing card as they enter. They then have to sit at the table that corresponds to that card's suit (so if you receive the king of clubs, you sit at the "clubs" table).

Personally, I like this activity. It keeps people from the same company from lumping themselves together at a single table. It's better for them and it's better for any other poor soul who might have been caught at the table with them. The only downside is if you invited a guest whom you wanted to sit next to. At that point you'll have to decide whether you will disregard the "game" or not. Don't worry. They rarely have hulking security guards on hand to put you in your place.

Advantages:

1. Random seating breaks up cliques and people who tend to sit with their own company.
2. Gives you the opportunity to meet new people who might not normally be in your circle.

Disadvantages:

1. Some people will refuse to play and insist on sitting with their own clique anyway.

2. You might become separated from your guest with whom you had hoped to partner network.

Tactics:

1. Be ready to meet new people (but you had already done that, right?).
2. If you want to connect with someone specifically, do so before the seated portion of the event takes place.

ONE-TO-ONE RAFFLE

The important point to remember is that the networking event is a great place to meet new people. The best time and place to continue developing those relationships is later at a one-to-one meeting (otherwise known as "breakfast," "lunch," "coffee," "high tea," — you get the point).

I've been to several events — usually Referrals Passing Groups or internal department meetings – where they take this realization one step further. Everyone puts a card in a basket. Then each person in turn selects one card to schedule a one-to-one meeting with that other person. This means that each time a group runs this activity; each participant has the opportunity to develop stronger connections with two other people in the group — the person they chose and the person who chose them.

If the attendees take it seriously, this is a great activity to encourage good networking. Many people aren't comfortable with the follow-up portion of the networking process. They feel as if they are intruding or perhaps they aren't sure which of all the people they've met they should reach out to. This "game" takes all that guessing out of the equation.

By the way, when you do pick someone's card, you should connect with them immediately to schedule the one-to-one before you walk out the door. It will save a lot of wasted time and effort later.

If you are visiting an event that has one of these activities scheduled, make sure you, as a guest, are allowed to play. Most groups won't have a problem with it, but you don't want to step on the culture of a group from which you hope to gain benefit later.

Advantages:

1. You have an excuse to have deeper conversations with other members of the group.
2. Developing stronger connections between members strengthens the group.
3. You can connect with members whom you might not otherwise have a chance to meet.

Disadvantages:

1. If the person who picks your card doesn't take it seriously, you miss out on connecting with them.
2. Technique works only with relatively small groups — ten to forty or so.

Tactics:

1. Verify that you are eligible to play.
2. Connect with whomever you pick before you walk out the door.
3. Try to do the same with whoever picks you.

PAY-A-DOLLAR BRAG SESSION

I haven't run into this one often but, just in case you see it, you should be prepared. I've most often seen it at smaller service club meetings, such as small-town Rotaries, but, again, that doesn't mean you won't see a similar activity elsewhere. The Brag Session is similar to the Pass the Microphone activity in that each person in turn has the opportunity to address the group. In this case, though, the group "passes the hat" — a basket, bowl, or even an actual hat — in which the potential speaker places a nominal donation — usually a dollar or two — in order to be allowed to talk about exciting updates happening for them or their business. Think of it as a paid advertisement.

The rules for this activity are similar to the Pass the Microphone activity. The money raised goes to help the organization or its interests — as I mentioned, this is often done in service-oriented groups. Keep it short and within whatever limits the organizer sets. Be aware that this activity might be limited to members of the group. If you are attending as a guest, ask your host what's expected. Often these messages can be personal in nature — births, marriages, new jobs — but as long as you aren't putting the hard-sell on your fellow attendees, you should be able to mention good news associated with your professional life. Again, ask the host what is expected.

Believe it or not, this is actually a really good activity. Depending on the limitations, you can talk about your business and what you are looking for. You can be personal, so people are getting to know the real you. You get to brag, but because you are putting your hard-earned money into the till, the other attendees will see that you are supporting the group directly and actively.

Advantages:

1. You tell the group about yourself and ask for what you need.
2. Depending on the message, you present yourself as a person.
3. You show yourself as an active supporter of the group's interests.

> **Disadvantages:**
> 1. Depending on the group, this might be a members-only benefit.
> 2. It costs money (but not much).
>
> **Tactics:**
> 1. Verify that you are eligible to play.
> 2. Prepare what you are going to say ahead of time.
> 3. Make sure you have money in your pocket.
> 4. Listen to others, take notes, and look for ways you can help.

THE BAD

A few activities that I've run into do *not* make for good networking. At best they are a waste of time. At worst, they reinforce bad networking behaviors. Still, these activities exist, and you might run into them on occasion, hence it's best to be beware – and prepare.

PASS YOUR CARD

The first of the "limited networking" activities is called "Pass Your Card." Basically, you grab a stack of your cards and pass it around the table so each person can grab one. I guess the idea is that the other attendees are going to pass your name along to potential prospects for you. This *does* work for closed networking groups where you want to pass along a referral to the other members. The reason it works, though, is that you've already put in the effort to know the other members of the group. You've already developed the relationship that is the basis of all networking.

For all other types of groups, at the end of the day you end up with a handful of cards for people whom you might not know at all. Certainly you won't know them well enough to pass them referrals yet. If I have a choice, I will usually skip playing this game. As far as I'm concerned except in the situation of a Leads Passing Group, it's a waste of cards.

If you do find yourself playing, do whatever you can to create a personal connection to the people represented by the cards you receive. Perhaps it was the person you chatted with over coffee before the event formally started. Maybe it was the gentleman who greeted you at the door. Whatever it is, make it as personal and as memorable as it can be. If you don't you're merely making a cold call for all they're concerned.

Advantages:

1. You get a handful of business cards.
2. The cards might encourage you to reach out to a potential connection.
3. You can practice your cold-calling technique.

Disadvantages:

1. You get a handful of business cards for people you've never met.
2. You have no connection with the people represented by the cards unless you interact with them before you leave the meeting.

Tactics:

1. Avoid taking part in this activity if you can. Give your cards out to those who take a genuine, personal interest in you. Otherwise, you might as well throw your cards in the trash.
2. Bring enough cards for everyone. Find out from your host how many you might need.
3. Take cards for those in whose services you might be interested or those whom you were going to follow up with anyway.

BUSINESS CARD COLLECTION RACE

Speaking of a waste of cards, I've once or twice been in the presence of a Business Card Collection Race. The idea of this one is literally to collect the most business cards in a fairly short time limit (usually about two or three minutes). This process completely dehumanizes the networking goal of creating relationships. The "winners" of this game are those who "wasted" the least amount of time finding out more about other people, asking what they do, or even saying hello. At the end of it, once again, you have nothing to show except a hand-ful of cards with names that you can't connect to faces (unless one is actually on a card). The only people who can really benefit from this game are the printers who provide cards to the attendees.

Advantages:

1. You get a handful of business cards.
2. For a few moments, you get to appreciate the world of panhandling except, instead of pocket change, you are begging for business cards — which in this case are worthless.

Disadvantages:

1. You get a handful of business cards for people to whom you probably haven't even said hello.
2. Completely misses the point of networking — to develop relationships.

Tactics:

1. Avoid taking part in this activity if you can. Give your cards out to those who take a genuine, personal interest in you.

2. Bring enough cards for everyone. Find out from your host how many you might need.

> 3. Find others in the group of a like mind, stand quietly to the side, and get to know each other.

FIND YOUR MATCH

This one sounds good on the surface. In fact, you might think it sounds a lot like Icebreaker Worksheet above, but it can end up backfiring. I've seen this one done at large mixer-style events. The idea is that, as you walk into an event, you receive two nametags. One has your name on it as usual. The other has a word or a mark or a paragraph. Your goal is to locate your matching nametag.

One time when I played this game, we were each given tags that had words and phrases associated with the sponsor's business, and the matching tag had the (sometimes quite long) definition. The first problem is caused by the fact that people tend to wear their nametags on their chests. Not to be crass, but staring at another's chest in a mixed-gender meeting is not the best way to make any-one comfortable with starting a long-term professional relationship. At a different event, the organizers had brought in a business that specialized in activities like this. In this case, each person received either a lock or a key. The goal was to find the match. It felt a little odd, though, to be propositioning each person I met with, "Let's see if my key fits your lock."

Ignoring the salacious overtones, this activity has two major flaws. First, people have a tendency to rush from person to person looking for their match without actually talking to anyone. Not the result you are looking for. The other is that the matching qualities have nothing to do with the people involved. They don't encourage developing an actual relationship with the other person because, really, you don't have to share any information about yourself to play (or even to win). My suggestion? Get a drink and chat with anyone else who doesn't want to play such a silly game.

Advantages:

1. Depending on the specific activity, it might simply be fun.

Disadvantages:

1. Purpose of the game misses the point of networking — to find out more about other people and develop relationships.
2. Implementation of the game can lead to inappropriate situations.

Tactics:

1. Find others in the group of a like mind, stand quietly to the side, and get to know each other.

WIN, LOSE, OR DRAW

What I have presented in this chapter is only a partial list of possible activities that might cause you to adapt your goals and style to better succeed at the event. This is one of the major reasons why you should be reaching out to your host or to the event organizer at the beginning of the event, or even before it begins. You need to be aware of what will be happening and decide on your strategy ahead of time.

The most important idea to remember in all this is, while it is fun to win, in those occasions when there is a named winner, be sure that winning actually accomplishes the goals you want to achieve by attending the event. If you don't see it happening that way, adapt your goals or your approach to better set yourself up for success.

CHAPTER

10

WINGMAN OR WET BLANKET? HOW TO NETWORK WITH A PARTNER

"Alone we can do so little; together we can do so much."

~ Helen Keller

You now have a good feel for the event and how to navigate it. Next we'll talk about a technique that if done properly could double your networking effectiveness. If done poorly, on the other hand, it could reduce that effectiveness to zero.

That technique is inviting a guest, otherwise known as "partner networking."

As we look at this powerful networking tactic, we have to look at specific concepts to make sure we are getting the most out of it.

WINGMAN OR WET BLANKET?
HOW TO NETWORK WITH A PARTNER

IN THIS SECTION YOU'LL...

- Learn three signs of partner networking failure.
- Discover eight benefits of having a good wingman.
- Pinpoint who would make a good partner.
- Develop specific partnering strategies.

At the very least, you want to avoid following the path that leads to wasting your time. Take a deeper look at...

THREE SIGNS OF PARTNER NETWORKING FAILURE

I see it every time I attend a business gathering. You see it, too. Whether it's a Chamber of Commerce breakfast, an after-hours reception with the local chapter of your trade association, or the weekly meeting of your Referral Passing Group, you look around and most folks are speaking with the same people they spoke with last time, and the time before that, and the time before that. What they are doing is not partner networking.

It might not even be *effective* networking.

If you find yourself with the same people at every gathering, be sure you've got a plan on how to help each other make new connections. Be mindful if any of the following is happening:

1. **You are trying to have a deep, one-to-one conversation with that other person.** Even if you agreed ahead of time, this probably isn't the best venue. Networking events are usually noisy and you will be constantly interrupted by other attendees. If you really want to forge a stronger connection with that other person, you are better off skipping the event and going for coffee.

2. **You are ignoring everyone else at the event.** Yes, you are probably more comfortable talking with your buddy, but that shouldn't be your goal. Networking events are opportunities to meet new people. Until you've reached the networking goal you set for this gathering, prolonged chatting with someone you already know is a luxury — like going to the buffet table.

3. **You are using them as an excuse to skip your networking goals.** You want a "wingman," not a "wet blanket," as a partner. You want someone to make your networking more effective, not cling to you and prevent you from getting your work done. Of course, it's nice not to leave them all on their own, but better to have them join in the fun at your side.

Let me repeat: Taking time to chat with people you already know here is not inherently ineffective. If you are going to spend the whole event together, though, they need to be an asset in your efforts to make better use of your time. You simply need to be careful that "partner networking" doesn't turn into "hanging out with your buddy."

EIGHT BENEFITS OF HAVING A GOOD WINGMAN

Now you know the warning signs of a failed attempt at partner networking. The question is: Is it even worth it? What sorts of benefits could you gain from having a "wingman"?

- **Moral Support.** Do you remember that first junior high school dance and how uncomfortable and awkward you felt walking into the room? Wasn't it a lot easier to walk in with a friend? Face it. We haven't changed that much since junior high. It's still a lot easier walking into a crowded room with a partner than it is walking in alone.

WINGMAN OR WET BLANKET?
HOW TO NETWORK WITH A PARTNER

- **Easier Access.** For most people, approaching a group (even if it's only two other people) when you are a singleton makes you feel like you are at a disadvantage. They already have a connection and you automatically feel like an outsider. When you have a wingman, you are bringing your own "group" along and can step into the situation on a more equal footing.

- **Accountability.** Do you know why people who are serious about getting fit choose to have workout partners? That's right! They do it because it's easy to break a promise to yourself, but harder to break it to someone else. A partner makes it more likely that you'll show up to sweat. Likewise, in networking, if you plan to attend a given event, you are less likely to blow it off if you know your buddy will be waiting for you.

- **Accountability, again.** One of the most powerful steps I ever took, one that has led to my success in business, was finding an accountability partner. Each time we talk, I have to commit to accomplishing certain tasks to grow my business. I know that I'm far more likely to get these tasks done when I have to report my status on our next phone call. When it comes to a business gathering, remember those goals you came up with when you were preparing for the event? If you share those goals with each other, you can each report on how well you did at the end of the day — and you are more likely to have met with success.

- **Education.** In almost every group you attend, you will encounter that one person who rocks the world as a networker. They know everyone and everyone knows them. They make the whole process look completely effortless. Especially if you are still feeling awkward about your networking technique, these might be the folks with whom you should partner. An experienced networker can teach the novice a lot about good networking practice by merely being a good example.

- **Coverage.** You've heard of "divide and conquer," right? While I don't normally like to use such aggressive phrases when talking about the process of relationship development, it does apply here. With two of you, you can cover more of the room and meet more potential additions to your networks.

- **Introductions.** Sometimes introducing yourself to another person can feel a little like you're bragging: "*I'm* Greg Peters. *My* business is The Reluctant Networker. *I* help people ...." Obviously, it's all about you and most people feel uncomfortable tooting their own horns. If someone else introduces you, though, they can brag about you and tell the other person why you are so great without your having to appear boorish. Obviously, this strategy works if one of you attended this event in the past, but it can work when you use one of the "split" strategies we'll talk about below — where you each spend time meeting people whom you can later introduce to each other.

- **Strengthen your relationship with each other.** Several of my best friendships in the whole world came about because of projects we worked on together. This is natural because in a good partnership, you are each looking out for the other's benefit — which is exactly how we build strong connections.

With all these benefits it almost doesn't make sense to ever attend an event alone. That said who should you invite to your next business gathering? After all, not everyone is going to be a great partner.

WHO WOULD MAKE A GREAT PARTNER?

As long as you follow good partnership strategy, you have a wide group of people from whom you can choose a potential teammate. You can invite a coworker, an employee, a friend, a family member, or even a client. In order to be successful, though, you need to look for more than simply a warm body with a pulse.

Here are five qualities to consider when selecting your wingman:

1. **The partner fits the venue and vice versa.** It should be obvious, but make sure your potential partner has experience to gain. Will they have access to clients? To people who can connect them with clients? Do they need vendors or employees and will they be represented at this event? You want this experience to be valuable for your partner. If they are trying to focus on international import/export firms, probably the local Chamber won't be as useful for them as it is for you. For a local residential real estate agent, though, that Chamber breakfast might be just what they need. This leads to the second quality...

2. **The partner met with you at least twice.** If you haven't met with them at least a couple of times, then you won't have enough familiarity with their business or personal needs. If you can't remember their company, position, and whether they are married, you probably don't have a strong enough connection yet.

3. **The partner worked or met with you *recently*.** Even if you've met with them several times, if it's been six months since the last time you had a good chat, you'll be tempted to spend all of your time talking with each other and catching up on the latest happenings. As I've said before, this isn't bad when you are sitting down together for coffee. It's just not effective in a crowded room and you are missing out on

other opportunities. The purpose of partner networking is to work together as a team to meet *other people*.

4. **They share your networking beliefs.** Here's one of those math story problems for you: Two people get into a car in Detroit. One thinks they are driving to New York City. The other thinks they are driving to Chicago. What are the chances that either of them is going to end up happy? Similarly, as partners in networking, you have to be going in with similar goals. Even if you both choose to focus on sales (an ineffective approach, as we've already seen), as long as you are both heading in that direction, you've got at least a chance of success. Even better if you are both working toward the same ultimate goal of extending your network through serving others.

5. **They are trustworthy with the Little Things.** Maybe your relationship hasn't progressed to the point where you are comfortable lending them your car, but you at least need to know that you can trust them to show up on time and be presentable. As partners you reflect each other. In fact, this is one reason you should be reaching out to them ahead of time. Let them know what information you've gathered about the event so they can be as prepared as you are.

Remember that most of the time you will only attend one or two events with a given partner. The primary purpose of these partnerships is for one of you to introduce a desirable networking venue to the other.

Conceivably, though, nothing is standing in your way of having a regular partner to help you keep on track with your networking practice, just as a workout partner can help you keep on track with your fitness goals.

SUCCESSFUL PARTNERING STRATEGIES

You probably have one or two people in mind whom you could invite to be a partner at the next networking event. Next you need a strategy. Depending on what you are trying to achieve, you may want to consider different plans of attack:

1. **Split, Then Socialize.** You and your partner meet up at the beginning of the event. You then each spend part of the event doing your regular networking. After you have achieved your networking goals, you can get back together and socialize. In addition to moral support (which all of the strategies provide), the only other of the eight benefits it provides is accountability. Still, it can work fine especially if you don't know each other very well yet.

2. **Split, Seek, Then Socialize.** The second plan is similar to the first, in that each of you does your own networking separately. This time, though, you'll each keep an eye out for people whom your partner might benefit from meeting. In fact, you should make your partner's goal a part of *your* networking goal for the event. Since you've already gotten to know each other outside the gathering, you should each have a good idea of whom the other is seeking. After you each complete your own networking, you then take time to introduce each other to those potentially good connections. After all that, the two of you can sit back and socialize.

3. **Follow the Leader.** The next strategy follows a mentoring focus. This approach is especially useful in situations where one of the partners is either new to networking in general or new to this particular group. With this course of action, the two partners stay together for most of or the entire event. The more experienced partner spends most of his time introducing the newbie to other members of the

group. In addition, if asked, he can coach the novice on effective networking skills. The downside of this practice is that the more experienced partner will end up not getting in as much of his own networking in favor of building the connection with the less experienced one. The partners will also cover less of the room since they will spend the event together.

4. **Full Tandem.** Similar to the Follow the Leader approach, Full Tandem networking involves staying together for the duration of the event. In this case, though, the partners are on an equal footing and may split the time focusing on each person's goals in turn. Using this technique, you will have less coverage than if you split up, but at times it is easier for a tandem team to break into an existing group. The one danger with this plan is that if you aren't careful you might find yourself standing and chatting with your partner instead of trying to connect with other people in the room.

5. **The Hybrid.** Finally, you could use a combination of the other strategies. Maybe you start out in a mentoring focus and then, as the less-experienced partner gets more comfortable, you might split up and each try to complete your separate goals.

Working in concert with a partner, you can make an event doubly effective. The main lesson to remember, no matter which strategy you use, is to ensure you and your partner discuss it ahead of time. You don't want the plan to be a surprise for either of you. You both want to be on the same page when you walk through the doors so you have the best chance of making your partnership pay off.

REVIEWING THE JOURNEY

That brings us to the end of Part 2. Looking back at the points of interest along the way, you should now:

- Be practicing the techniques to free yourself from the limitations of the "Stranger Danger" mindset.

- See the benefits of showing up early at the networking event.

- Have a plan for what activities to do surrounding networking opportunities.

- Be prepared for the different types of networking events and have a plan on how to be effective at each.

- Know how to navigate various networking games and activities that you might encounter at the event.

- Understand the benefits of having a networking partner.

- Have strategies to make your partnership more successful.

Now all we have to do is work on the most important skill when it comes to networking: Creating connections through conversation.

PART

3

STARTING POWERFUL CONNECTIONS WITH POISE AND GRACE

"Whether a plane to Singapore, a subway in Manhattan, or the streets of Cincinnati, I search for meaningful conversation wherever I may travel. Without it, I believe we lose the ability to not only understand others, but more importantly, ourselves."

~ Dhani Jones

Here we are in Part 3. In Part 1, you learned about how to prepare yourself — your mental focus, and your physical toolkit — to be ready to show up and be the best connector you can be at the networking function. In Part 2, we covered what to expect during the event and tactics you can use to make them pay off. In this section, we're going to work on the most important technique for creating powerful connections.

Making conversation.

Hey, wait a minute! Come back here. This isn't anywhere near as scary or difficult as it sounds. By the time we're done, you'll have a simple set of techniques to help you be more effective and have a lot more fun in the process.

STARTING POWERFUL CONNECTIONS
WITH POISE AND GRACE

In fact, I wish someone had taken me aside when I first started networking to tell me how easy conversation could be. Really, all you need to do is keep in mind one of the fundamental rules of networking: **It's almost never about you. It's almost always about them.** If you gain nothing else from this section, keep that one dictum in mind. The more you focus on them and their comfort, the more you ask great questions that show an interest in who they are and what they do, the more you truly *are* interested, intrigued, and fascinated by those around you, the easier and more productive the conversation will be.

The conversational skills you learn in this section will help you leave your fears out in the car and let you start making powerful connections with poise and grace.

CHAPTER

11

BE THE ONE THEY WANT TO MEET

"A real conversation always contains an invitation. You are inviting another person to reveal herself or himself to you, to tell you who they are or what they want."

~ David Whyte

Here's the mistake that most people make in conversation at a networking event: They forget about first impressions. Suppose you and I met a moment ago. If I spend the entire time talking about myself, you probably wouldn't be particularly impressed or want to continue talking with me for any significant length of time. Now imagine how much worse it would be if I spent the whole time talking about my business. Still not bad enough? How about if I started pressuring you to buy from me?

Are you thinking you'd be looking for an exit at about that point? I wouldn't blame you.

I mentioned the statistics on earlier. Depending on who you believe, you have between two seconds and a minute before the other person will make a snap judgment about the kind of person you are — good, bad, or other.

If you come across as a strong-arm salesperson in those first few moments, people will treat you as such — they'll probably run. What you want is for that other person to view you as a valuable connection. You want them to look forward to chatting with you.

You want to make conversations, not pitches.

IN THIS SECTION YOU'LL...

- Discover the dangers of the sales mindset.
- Look at the numbers behind networking as relationship development.
- Examine a few of the best practices with respect to business cards.

DANGERS OF THE SALES MINDSET

We touched on this problem briefly back in Part 1, but examine, again, the challenge of focusing on sales.

Imagine you're at a networking event and find yourself chatting with two people. One of them is a perfect client for you. Oh, she doesn't realize it yet, but with a little careful questioning, she'll discover that she needs about a hundred of your widgets. Wouldn't that be a great contract? What about the other person? He's nice and all, but he doesn't have any use for widgets.

Who should you focus your attention on?

Oh, did I mention that the second individual is married to a corporate buyer who is looking for a supplier who can provide one thousand widgets per month for the next five to ten years? Does that change your answer?

You can't know who is going to connect you with your best opportunities. Sure, you might luck out and happen to run into someone who desperately needs your widgets, but the chances are vanishingly slim. If you focus on building good relationships, finding prospects will take care of itself.

NETWORKING BY THE NUMBERS

Let's look at completely made-up numbers that nonetheless illustrate what I'm talking about. **Warning**: This does involve math. Remain calm. Don't panic. This isn't anywhere near as complicated as those story problems where two people jump on trains going in opposite directions and you have to somehow figure out what they eat for lunch.

First, we'll make an assumption: On average you can meet and have a substantive conversation with about one hundred people over the course of a year. Yes, a few people can do more and to others that number sounds unbelievably unachievable. Stick with it, though, as it makes the math a lot easier.

FOCUSING ON PROSPECTIVE CLIENTS (I.E., "SALES")

First, look at the case for prospecting for clients at the event. Over the course of the year, you meet those hundred people. Suppose that you are just an *amazing* salesperson. You're able to take them through your sales process and close a full ten percent. By the way, if you don't have a lot of sales experience, ten percent is knocking it out of the ballpark. According to statistics I've read from a variety of sources, cold calling usually results in a two to six percent success rate (depending on what you mean by success). Assume, though, that you can actually achieve a ten percent close rate. Doing a little bit of math, we get ten percent of one hundred or ten sales over the course of a year.

Hey, ten sales is darned good, right? I wouldn't turn down ten sales. Get out those business cards and start selling at events!

Whoa, there. Slow it down a little and look at the other option.

FOCUSING ON RELATIONSHIPS (I.E., "NETWORKING")

Once again you meet one hundred people, but this time you try to make a connection. Now you *will* have a little bit more work because you have to develop the relationships (though probably not significantly more than you'd have to do to take people through a sales process). Assume only about a fifth of them, or about twenty, make it into your long-term network.

Here's where the power of a network comes in. According to the Guinness Book of World Records, Joe Girard is the best salesperson in the world. Between 1963 and 1978 he sold over 13,000 cars at a Chevy dealership in Michigan. He became such a great salesperson not because he had amazing sales techniques, but because he understood the nature of connections. He came up with the Law of 250. According to this law, every person, on average, knows about 250 people who they'd invite to their wedding or who would show up to their funeral. Doing the math, assuming they're average, your twenty new friends know somewhere in the area of 5,000 people (that's 20 times 250). By creating these new relationships, **you've effectively expanded your extended network by 5,000 people!**

Next, focus on those twenty new friends. Because of the relationships you've forged, these folks are looking out for you. If any one of their connections might need your services, they'll probably refer those folks to you.

Assume further that a mere half a percent of these people in the extended network need our help. That's .005 X 5,000 or *twenty-five* people who might like to buy from us.

Twenty-five?

So the choice is ten possible sales or twenty-five people who want to buy from you? The math favors that whole relationship thing. Shocking, right?

MORE NUMBERS

The numbers aren't over yet. Look at what happens next year. For the person who focuses on sales, they then get to repeat this process, starting with having conversations with one hundred people and ending up with ten sales.

What happens with you, the person who focused on relationships? You go through your whole process of developing twenty new networking connections and ending up with twenty-five people buying from you. Guess what else, though? Remember the twenty friends from last year? They are still in your network and could quite easily still be sending you business. The only bad news is, if this process keeps up, sooner or later, you won't have time to do a lot of selling because too many people will be calling you, wanting to buy.

Here's another set of numbers, just for the fun of it. Imagine a scale from zero to ten representing the sales process where zero is "I met you in the past few minutes" and ten means "I signed a contract with you." Where do you suppose those ten potential sales start out for the guy who focuses on selling? Zero, right? I mean, he just met them at the networking event and now he has to take them all the way from zero to ten. What about those people from your extended network who are connected with you because they want to buy what you have to sell? They've already been selected by your network. They're probably an eight, nine, or even a ten (and, yes, I have had referral partners do exactly that for me).

REMEMBER YOU ARE ALREADY IN THE RIGHT PLACE

Even ignoring the numbers, when it comes to your networking focus, here's another aspect to consider: You are already in the right place.

Even if you aren't actively selling, people may say that you should spend at least a little time deciding whether the person you are talking with can be of benefit to you. I have to disagree for a couple of reasons. First, this kind of self-serving conversation will get in the way of creating connection. You've probably been on the receiving end of this conversation before. No matter how skillfully that other person tried to disguise it, couldn't you tell what they were doing? That probing process feels unnatural and it probably left a bad taste in your mouth.

The second reason is, it's unnecessary. Remember all that work you did to prepare for the event? Part of that effort was to determine if this event or this group was the right one for you. You already know that the person you are chatting with is either in your target market or likely *knows* someone who is in your target market. The question isn't whether they *can* help you, but, rather, whether they *want* to help you.

And having a focus on creating and strengthening relationships is more likely to sway them to your side of that equation.

DON'T LET YOUR BUSINESS CARD GET IN THE WAY OF CONNECTION

We want to create connections. Great! Be careful, though. If you follow the old-school way of networking, now it's all about making sure everyone in the room has your business card. Unfortunately, a lot of new networkers learn this and can't understand why it isn't paying off for them. We talked a bit about cards back in Part 1, but let's look at business card culture to see where your strategy might be going wrong.

When I first started networking, I would show up at the event — the Chamber networking lunch, for example. I would do the best I could, mixing and mingling with the other attendees. I would get so excited when, after chatting for a few minutes, someone would ask me for one of my business cards.

Naturally, I would present them with my card (sometimes two!) and then I would return home with the glow of success all about me. Yes, sir, business was really about to take off! For the next several days, I would look forward with anticipation to their call.

Of course, no one ever (and I mean *ever*) called.

Unfortunately, truly great networkers are few and far between. These are the folks who, when they ask for your card, actually will follow up— and I don't mean simply putting it in the pile on their desk. Their actions align with their intent and they have a system to support it.

The rest of the folks who ask (about ninety-eight percent) may or may not intend to call you. They may only ask to be polite or they may want to give you one of their cards in exchange. Either way, handing them a card is a lot like throwing it away (which they will eventually do when they can no longer remember where they got it or who you are).

Instead of depending on the kindness of strangers, if you find someone with whom you would like to continue the conversation beyond the event, *you* ask for *their* card. Then — and here's the mark of a true networker — *you* take the initiative to contact them with the purpose of learning about them and, ultimately, develop a long-term, mutually-beneficial relationship.

Heck, even better, ask for their card and, before you walk away from each other, schedule your next meeting. Then you don't need to worry about contacting them later.

Remember, the most valuable card at the networking event is the one you get from someone else. Then it's up to you to turn that brief connection into a deeper connection.

Please, don't misunderstand what I'm saying about handing out your business card. I do think you should have them handy, and if someone asks, certainly give it to them — after all, no need to make them feel bad. Don't get into the habit of giving it out if they haven't asked. It's a waste of your cards and their good will.

"TWO OR MORE" TACKINESS

As long as we're talking about business cards, we should probably address one other topic that I mentioned before in passing.

In the years that I've been networking, I've occasionally noticed a practice that I learned myself when I was starting out. In retrospect the behavior is kind of strange. Let me set the scene. I'd be at a Chamber lunch or a member reception — the exact event wasn't particularly important. Imagine the sounds of dozens of people chatting together in the background. I'm making my rounds at the gathering. I meet someone new and we have a nice, if short, conversation. We are connecting nicely for a first meeting and then they politely ask for my card.

I hand them two.

Someone somewhere had told me that this was a good idea. After all, that way they'd have one for themselves and one for another person, right?

Think that through.

A referral by its very nature is the act where one person effectively lends another person their reputation. If I tell you that Bob Smith is a great accountant and you decide to use him, you're doing so because you trust my judgment. If Bob messes up your taxes not only do you distrust Bob, but *my* reputation becomes tarnished.

So what are the chances that someone you just met and spoke with for a total of five minutes will be willing to lend you their reputation?

After you've met for coffee a time or two and you *wait until they ask*, then you can pass them two cards (and when I say "they ask" I mean they specifically ask for more than one card). Remember, passing more than one card implies that you are expecting that other person to refer business to you. If your relationship isn't at that level yet, then you're only succeeding in making them uncomfortable and that's not good networking practice.

Keep the extra cards in your pocket. Your printer might not thank you, but everyone else will.

Now that we've dealt with what to do with your business cards and how not to let them get in the way of what you are supposed to be doing. Let's talk about what you are supposed to be doing.

Making connections.

CHAPTER 12

TALKING WITH STRANGERS

"We're our own dragons as well as our own heroes, and we have to rescue ourselves from ourselves."

~ Tom Robbins

Here's where most people fall down. You see them whenever you attend a networking event. They lurk at the back of the room. They're the first ones to the buffet line. They pick a table that has no one sitting at it. They eat their food, listen to the speaker, then are the first ones out the door.

You might wonder to yourself what they are doing.

They're waiting.

They're waiting for someone to come over and say hello. They're waiting for their clients to walk up to them. They're waiting for this whole painful networking torture to be over.

They're waiting for "networking" to happen to them.

At this point, two thoughts should come to your mind:

1. **Don't be them.** Control your own networking destiny. Seek out the people with whom you want to talk. Make plans to meet tomorrow or the next day. Sit at the table that has only one or two seats left. First, accomplish your networking goal. Then sit and relax.

2. **Help them.** That "sitter" is probably a new networker. They don't know that they need a networking goal. They desperately want someone to rescue them. Help them out. You will be a superhero in their eyes.

Sitting at a networking event is fine during the presentation (if there is one) and up to ten minutes before. Otherwise you should be on your feet making connections and meeting new people. Don't be the person who walks out of the gathering saying to yourself, "What a waste of time. I couldn't find anyone good to talk with," when in fact you never looked in the first place.

Of course, as we talked about before, most people have an aversion to talking with strangers. It's part of our programming from way back.

And that's the danger.

If you are consciously or subconsciously avoiding talking with people you don't know, it's going to be hard to extend your network. After all, the people you know are *already* a part of your network.

Since meeting strangers is sort of the first step, you need to crush this "stranger danger" pattern and get it out of your head (at least for the time you're at the event). Back in Chapter 5 we talked about adopting the "host mindset" and that's a good start. What else could you do? Here are three areas you can focus on to give you confidence the next time you "welcome a guest."

Let's take a look at each of these in turn.

IN THIS SECTION YOU'LL...

- Become aware of the resources you have to offer.
- Develop curiosity about the people you meet.
- See opportunities to practice when it doesn't matter.

KNOW THYSELF

A couple of the excuses I hear all the time about networking and passing referrals are "I don't have time to find referrals for *myself*, let alone the people in my network!" and "I'm just a student/new hire/retiree/technician/widget salesperson. I don't have anything to offer." I can see where they're coming from if they believe that the only way to be of service is to secure a big contract for their networking partners.

Fortunately, that's not the way it works. In reality it's the little gestures, relatively cost-free to you (in terms of time and effort), that can mean the most to your connections, given a little bit of timing. You simply need to be aware of what you do have to offer.

- **Are they traveling to a place you've been before?** Lend or give them your travel books that are gathering dust on your shelves.

- **Are they looking for new employees?** Introduce them to the head of Career Services at the local community college.

- **Are they looking for more clients?** Send them that article that gave you the breakthrough in your own prospecting.

- **Are they looking for a nice restaurant for their anniversary?** Tell them where you and your spouse went last. Oh, and tell them where the good seats are, too.

- **Are they feeling confused about their next steps?** Lend an ear. Occasionally, that's all it takes.

For most relationships, it's not the grand gestures that build the strongest connections. You didn't develop your personal friendships by sending them on a cruise. It was the little things over time. The more you network, the more connections you make, the stronger relationships you build, the more resources you have to offer to those you meet. Networking makes you a more valuable networker.

Grab a piece of paper (or the electronic equivalent). Start jotting down the names of all the people you know. If possible, include what they do, what special resources they might be able to call upon, and what they are looking for. If you don't know the answers to those questions, you've got an excuse to contact them. Do the same for yourself. Don't limit your list only to professional skills and services.

Look at all you have to offer that next person you meet and realize how lucky they are to be talking with you.

DEVELOP CURIOSITY

You've probably heard the old joke about the three most important qualities to look for when buying a house — location, location, location. In a similar manner, successful networking requires three qualities — curiosity, curiosity, curiosity.

I'm not talking about being curious whether the other person can buy from you or connect you with someone who can buy from you. Rather, what you need is a genuine interest and fascination with other people and how you can help them. This might not be easy for you. If you are of a more analytic or data-oriented nature or have a personality preference that focuses on the bottom line, you might see another person's personality quirks and personal history to be an irrelevant factor in achieving your ultimate goals.

When you accept, though, that your long-term success in life is largely dependent on the relationships you form over time, you might see it's worth the effort. You can't form those connections without being curious about the people around you and what they hope to achieve. Really, all you need to do is ask. Be interested in their past, their goals, and their mission. You might be surprised, but people enjoy talking with you when they are talking about themselves.

Curiosity may not have been so healthy for the proverbial cat, but without it, your networking value is the same as the real estate value of a nice house in the wrong part of town.

Be interested. Be fascinated. Be curious.

PRACTICE WHEN IT DOESN'T MATTER

Of course, making connections always matters, but somehow it feels like it matters more when you are at a "Networking Event." To get past that feeling, take every opportunity to talk with other people when the stress levels are lower. When could that be? How about starting with simple situations such as talking with the cashier at the grocery store or the salesperson who helps you pick out that nice new outfit? How about the person who waits on you at lunch? You are already communicating with them. Now you can make it a little more personal.

Some easy questions you might ask:

- **How are you doing today?** Yeah, not exactly original, but you have to start the conversation by showing that you really care, not just the perfunctory query that most people use.

- **How has business been?** Is that normal for this time of day? Let them be an expert.

- **How long have you worked here? What do you like best about working here?** Let them tell their story.

- If in a restaurant: **What's your favorite dish on the menu? Why?** Again, they get to be the expert.

- **Do you have any fun plans for the weekend/holiday?** Most people love to talk about their recreation/family and this is a good way to bring that out.

You'll be amazed at the conversations you'll have. One young cashier I spoke with told me that she was currently in college studying international relations with a goal of eventually working in the State Department or possibly even becoming the Secretary of State. Wow!

Be aware, not every person you talk with is going to be receptive. One or two will simply want you to be quiet so they can get their jobs done and get you sent along your way. In general, though, you'll notice that most folks are smiling before you leave. After all, how many people treat them as human beings?

And you are developing the conversational skills that will stand you in good stead when you walk through the doors of the next association chapter meeting.

You've got your "Host" hat on. You are aware of all you have to offer. You are looking at the folks around you with the eyes of the curious. You've even had a chance to practice when it wasn't important, and you are ready to start connecting. The next question is: Who should you approach and how?

CHAPTER

13

BREAKING IN AND BREAKING THE ICE

"Every crowd has a silver lining."

~ P. T. Barnum

I remember attending dances when I was at Van Hoosen Junior High (I think they call them "middle schools" now). Does this sound at all familiar to you?

It's the day of the dance. I never look forward to these embarrassing and degrading teenage rites of passage, but I feel like I'm supposed to go. I'm dressed up just enough to make me feel like I'm not being myself. After the final bell rings, I head to the cafeteria that some student group has decorated with streamers and balloons. I show my ticket and walk in.

I can see the cool kids already in groups out on the dance floor. They are all having a grand time. I look around for anyone I know, but most of my friends don't go to these types of social gatherings.

I don't know how to dance, so I slink over to the edge of the room and find a chair next to another group of kids who are chattering with each other and obviously enjoying themselves. Me? I sit there, bored, and hope that a person will walk up to me, say hello, and somehow miraculously make this a fun, exciting event.

No one does.

By the end, I can't wait to go home. What a huge waste of time and money this day has been. Later on that evening, when my mom asks how the dance went, what do I say?

"Fine."

If you change a few words in that story, does it sound like your experience with networking events, too? Wouldn't you like to change the story to be in with the "cool kids"? If so, the first step you have to take is stop hiding at the edge of the room. What do you do instead? Join groups of people and, yes, talk with them.

IN THIS SECTION YOU'LL...

- Learn why and how to approach the smallest group possible.
- Develop tactics to deal with special cases.
- Prepare yourself with your opening lines.

WHOM SHOULD YOU APPROACH AND HOW?

Standing at the edge of a large group of people — all apparently talking with each other — can be daunting. How do you break into the group?

The trick is to aim for the low-hanging fruit first. After all, as we discussed, you already know you are in the right place. Even if the next person you meet *isn't* the best-connected person in the room, they might *know* the best-connected one and who's to say they aren't worth knowing in their own right?

The trick is to look for the smallest group possible.

ONE PERSON

The smallest group, of course, is one. As you scan the room, keep your radar tuned for the wallflowers standing off on their own. Never pass up the chance to chat with one person. If you see that singleton standing off by himself (assuming he isn't talking on his cell phone), then you can maintain your "host attitude," walk up, and say "Hi." I'll occasionally say that they looked bored or lonely so I thought I would come over to say hello. Introduce yourself. Listen to their response and then strike up a conversation. A lot of times, if you see a person standing alone off to the side, it means that they are painfully uncomfortable with the situation, so you approaching them makes you the hero.

By the way, that person sitting alone isn't necessarily a bad person to get to know. She may simply be feeling a little overwhelmed. You never know who you might meet. I was working with an executive at a Fortune 500 company. She claimed to look for these singletons all the time. Once she sat down next to a gentleman and, after chatting with him for a few minutes, discovered that he was the President of a local bank — definitely a person who many of us would like to count among our network.

We should mention a special case here...

THE NEWBIE

Being in a group for a long time can pose a hidden danger. As you spend more time with the other members of the group, you build stronger and stronger relationships with them. That's good. Don't get me wrong. As you do that, however, you can have the tendency to spend all of your time with them and never pay attention to the new people who are trying out the group for the first time.

In addition to nurturing your existing relationships, be sure to take time for those newbies you see across the room. Doing this benefits a number of different parties.

1. **The Newbie.** Of course, it's good for the newbie to feel welcome. No one likes to feel all alone in a room full of people. You get to be his hero and that will give you a head start into a stronger long-term relationship — even if he doesn't stay with the group.

2. **The Event Organizers.** Setting up, breaking down, maintaining the agenda, scheduling speakers, arranging for the catering — event organizers have a lot of tasks to keep track of before, during, and after the event. If you are willing to greet new people and make them feel comfortable, you have taken one more worry off their plates. In fact, they probably wouldn't mind if you offered to be the quasi-official greeter. Ask them every now and then. Remember, the organizers are often among the best-connected people at the event. Having them think well of you certainly can't hurt.

3. **The Other Group Members.** Every group benefits from an infusion of new blood. If your efforts to welcome a newbie help lead her to become a new long-term member, you have given the group access to new ideas, new networking connections, and new enthusiasm.

4. **You.** Someone you've made feel welcome is more likely to open their network for the purpose of helping you. Since he's new, it's likely that he has access to hundreds or thousands of other people, several of whom might be your perfect clients.

Remember, at one point you were the new person walking into your first group event. You were nervous and didn't know who to talk with or what would be happening next. Now that you've become an integral part of the group and have built your extensive network, it is your moral imperative to reach out your hand to the current crop of newcomers.

And, really, for the cost of a smile, a handshake, and a simple willingness to help them fit in, you and everyone involved have so much to gain. It makes no sense not to make that extra effort.

That all said, what if you are in a room of rampant extroverts and there are no singletons to be seen? Simply follow our "smallest group" rule to the next step...

TWO PEOPLE

No one is standing alone. Next on the list to look for, and more difficult because you actually are breaking in, *are* groups of two people.

This one is a little more challenging. You need to read their body language to know how or whether to approach. For example, if they're shoulder to shoulder, facing the room, then feel free to walk up and say hello. Chances are they aren't having a private conversation and simply asking if you may join them should be sufficient.

If, on the other hand, they're squared off to each other (face to face), then they're usually having a private conversation, which you would be rude to interrupt. Interrupting is not good networking. If they're shoulder to shoulder facing away from the room, hunched over, and talking in low tones or whispers, they are probably planning a bank heist. You don't want to be in the middle of that!

All joking aside, the key here is to watch the body language and be respectful of the established conversation.

This situation has a special case, too. You might happen upon a conversational pairing, but one of the people is someone you already know. If you can catch your friend's eye, then he's likely to invite you to join them and make the necessary introductions. Of course, still keep an eye on the body language. Even your friends have a right to a private conversation.

THREE PEOPLE

Suppose that all of the singletons are people you've already met and the groups of two are all planning bank heists. Next up on the list will be groups of three. I met a young man at one of my live workshops who claimed that he actually loved to enter an existing three-way conversation. His method was to walk up, wait for a break, and then ask for permission to join. He said it was more efficient than meeting people one at a time.

I can see where he's coming from; provided you pay attention to the body language as you would with groups of two, this would probably work. My main concern is that it's harder to make a real connection with three people than it is with only one or two. It can lead to another problem, as well.

A many years ago at a Chamber of Commerce mixer, I found myself in a conversation with three other attendees. I found I had good chemistry with two of them and both of them would have been great long-term networking connections. The third? He was a nice guy, but we simply didn't "click." I was in a quandary. Should I ask for the cards from the two with whom I wanted to follow up and ignore the third? That would be rude. Should I ask for business cards from all three and discard the one I didn't want? That also seemed a bit impolite – and if he was friends with the others, might come back to haunt me. Of course, I could always try to catch up with the two "keepers" later in the mixer, but what if they left before I could reconnect?

In the end, I went with option two, collecting cards from all three. I ended up feeling guilty about it to this day. Did he realize I was only being polite? Did it taint my relationships with the others (neither of whom ended up as a long-term connection)?

These days I would go with option three. If I can't comfortably ask for their contact information or schedule a follow-up with them because others are present, I let it go. I'll try to reconnect before the end of the gathering or catch up with them at another event. If it never happens, that's okay. I will have plenty of other opportunities to connect and no one will feel left out.

FOUR OR MORE

If you have no other choice, I guess you can consider groupings of four or more people. The advantage of larger groups is that, as the number increases, it actually becomes easier to join in. The larger the group, the less likely it is that they are having a private conversation. The downside is that it becomes almost impossible to make connections with individuals — which is the whole purpose behind going to the event in the first place.

On the other hand, larger groups like this *can* become unstable and often break up into smaller groups of two or three. Remember, you can't control that process so don't count on it happening on your schedule.

SPECIAL CASES

Let's talk about a couple of special cases when it comes to breaking into groups.

FRIENDS

What if the group has people you already know in it? This situation can be a double-edged sword. On the one hand, having an acquaintance or friend already in the mix can make that initial approach a lot easier. On the other hand, you might be tempted to spend your time chatting with your friend instead of connecting with the new people in the group. If your goal is to reconnect with your existing network, that's fine, but you're probably missing out on great networking opportunities.

On a related note, this is another benefit of networking with a partner. It's easier to break into another group if you have a wing-man — especially if your partner is more experienced in this venue. In fact, I experienced this myself when I attended the National Speakers Association conference for the first time. At the beginning of the conference, I had made a brief contact with Bob Burg, one of my personal heroes. From that point on, whenever he saw me, he made a point of introducing me to fascinating people whom I might not otherwise have met.

SOMEONE YOU REALLY WANT TO MEET

One other special case came up during one of my live programs. The person wanted to know how to break into a conversation. I shared with him the same ideas we just talked about here, but he was dissatisfied with to the rule of not breaking into a "private" conversation. He asked, "But, what if you *really* want to meet one of those people?"

I don't remember exactly what I said at the time, but, in retrospect, here's what I wish I had said:

"Well, in that case, if you *really* want to meet a person, feel free to throw any rules of etiquette out the window. Push right up and elbow that other person out of the way so that you can get in contact with your target. Of course, there will be consequences."

Just as there will be consequences if I walk into Best Buy, grab a big screen TV off the shelf, and try to walk out with it. Just because I *really* want it, doesn't mean I get to ignore the rules of proper behavior.

Of course, even assuming you're following proper behavior, you should pause for a brief moment of reflection. You need to ask yourself, *"Why* is it so important that I meet this person?" If it's because someone else told you that this person could help you with a problem you have (and you're willing to pay for that assistance), okay. If you can connect them with someone from your network to their benefit, that's good, too.

If you *want* something from them (like money), forget it.

Most of the time when a person tells me that they *really* want to meet someone, what they mean is that they *really* want to sell to that person. Or maybe they want that person to refer them. If we're trying to connect with someone for the sole purpose of benefiting ourselves, we're placing ourselves in the role of "user."

Bad networking.

Remember the Golden Rule of Networking: **Use only those techniques on others that you would wish them to use on you.** I don't care who you are. No one wants to be interrupted in order to be sold to. Approach respectfully with a genuine interest in how you can help them (with no expectation of return) and I'm sure they will welcome you with open arms (or at least a firm handshake and a smile).

ICEBREAKERS

Congratulations! You've successfully broken into a group for the purpose of having a conversation. You just have to figure out how to kick it off.

I'm now going to share with you my ultimate, top-secret, never-fails opening line that took me years to discover. Now that I've started using it, though, it has kicked off numerous fantastic and often profitable relationships. Make sure no one is reading over your shoulder because we really don't want this to get out. Are you ready for it? Here it is:

"Hello."

I've used variations such as, "Hi," "Howdy," and "Good Morning." Yes, of course, I'm being serious. Honestly, this is conversation. All you have to do is act like a reasonable human being who is genuinely interested in meeting other people. The best way to convey this message is through a simple greeting.

I'll then offer a handshake and say, "My name's Greg." Occasionally I'll throw in my last name.

Silliness aside, the next step is where the conversation takes off and you might need to show finesse. Despite its reputation for being a boring and clichéd question to ask in a business setting, I like some variation on, "So what do you do?" Here's where the finesse comes in, again, assuming you are in a business-oriented gathering.

First, look for their nametag. If it has a business name on it, you could start out with, "I see you work at Filbert Brothers. What do you do there?"

If they don't have a nametag, then you want to be careful. Many people these days are networking because they're between jobs. Several of them are uncomfortable with this fact. Coming out and asking them "What do you do for a living?" might underscore this situation and put them in a "not okay" state. Instead, you might go with, "What industry are you in?" or "What line of work are you in?" or my personal favorite, "What's been keeping you busy lately?" Recognize their expertise. Don't dwell on their current situation.

If all else fails, a good stand-by is, "What brings you here today?" Almost anything they say can be a springboard into a larger conversation.

In a more social situation such as a party or wedding reception where people sometimes frown on "shop talk," you can use that last one, too. You might find out they're related to the bride, or old friends of the family. Either way, it's a start to the conversation.

What's that? Yes, you have initiated a "conversation." Don't panic. We're about to cover what to do next.

CHAPTER

14

HELP! I'M IN A CONVERSATION. NOW WHAT DO I DO?

"That's all small talk is — a quick way to connect on a human level — which is why it is by no means as irrelevant as the people who are bad at it insist. In short, it's worth making the effort."

~ Lynn Coady

Once you're in the conversation, whether it's a group of two or twenty, remember that your goal is to find out about the other people and then decide if you'd enjoy meeting them again. Chat, get cards if it makes sense, and then move on. Save the long conversations for when you are seated over coffee at a later date.

So what should you be prepared to talk about during this brief initial chat? Here's a little hint:

Don't talk — ask.

IN THIS SECTION YOU'LL...

- Develop a series of conversation-building questions to help you connect more easily.
- Learn the importance of your own curiosity.
- Find ways to end the conversation gracefully.

ASKING GOOD QUESTIONS

Your goal as a great networker is always to find ways to connect with the other person. That said, you will not be successful if you're spending all your time talking about yourself. Believe it or not, by seeking to discover more about *them*, they will begin to see *you* as the most interesting person they've met.

The trick is to ask open-ended, follow-up questions. Try asking about some of these topics:

THEIR OCCUPATION

Suppose in your initial efforts, you discover that they work for Filbert Brothers as a Widget Sales Representative. You can then follow up with:

- **"How did you get started?"** Most people are more than happy to tell the story of their success.

- **"What sort of challenges do you see in the upcoming year?"** You may discover a way you can help them right away — a great way to cement a strong relationship early.

- **"How long have you been doing that?"** If they've been doing it for a while, then the question **"How has the industry changed in the time you've been in it?"** allows them be an expert. In fact, if anyone has been doing the same work for longer than three years, I can almost guarantee that not only have there been changes, but they will have a strong opinion about it. When a person is speaking passionately about a topic, you're more likely to find out who they really are.

- **"What sort of exciting changes are going on in the industry right now?"** is another good one for the same reason.

Start with the "boring" question about what they do. Then by simply asking good follow-up questions — ones where they can't merely answer yes or no — you will keep the conversation going and allow them to talk about their favorite topic — themselves.

THEIR INTERESTS

Remember that you are trying to make a connection to another human being and, for most of us, our job or business is not the be-all and end-all of life. Shift the focus away from work.

- **"What do you like to do when you aren't doing accounting/ running the bank/selling widgets?"** I often ask this question in one-on-one meetings over coffee, but it works just as well at the event. This is what they are about as human beings.

- **"How long have you been doing that?"** or **"How did you get started with that hobby?"** A lot of the follow-up questions we were asking about their job or business apply here, too.

- If they start talking about their children, be careful. You want to show interest, but not be creepy. In general, let them lead. If you need to ask follow-up questions, ask about your conversation partner's experience, not about details of the children's lives. **"How *do* you fly to Japan and back with a four-year-old and an eight-year-old?"** is a good example of a safe follow-up (assuming the conversation was about travel with children).

Going beyond shop talk gives them an opportunity to be a person and not just a job. You might even find a common point of interest, which is a great way to connect. Strangers can become fast friends over a shared uncommon passion.

THEIR FUTURE

The third area we can talk about is their future. Remember, we aren't going too deep here. Try not to freak them out by asking them about their life's goals. Assuming this is a first meeting, start small.

- **"What are your plans for the upcoming month/season?"** Whether they share personal or business information, you'll find out about their goals and aspirations. These may be areas in which you can lend a hand.

- You can be more specific by asking about a particular area — especially one that might be personally interesting to you. **"Do you have any fun travel plans coming up?"**

- You still want to be ready with the follow-up. **"Really? I've never been to Italy. What made you choose that destination?"**

- If you want to stay focused on the professional side, you can always ask them about that. **"What are some of the big projects in your business this year?"** Especially as you become a better-connected networker, you may be able to introduce them to people or resources that might help them achieve those grand goals.

THE EVENT

If you aren't sure what you might have in common, start with the topic you *know* you have in common — the event you are attending.

- If this is a recurring event, ask them, **"Have you been to this event before?"**

- If they are new to the venue and you are the old hand, ask, **"What are you hoping to gain from being here?"** or even **"Who would you like to meet?"**

- If *they're* the more experienced one, ask, **"What do you like about this event?"** or **"What have you gained from attending?"** Not only will it give you information that will make your own networking more productive, but it will give them a chance to be the hero and rescue you.

- Finally, **"What other events do you attend in the area?"** which you can then follow up with **"Why?"** At the minimum, this question can point out other events that you might want to consider for yourself. As a bonus, it might let you know what other groups your conversation partner belongs to and even what his target market might be (which might lead you to being able to refer him at some later date).

Quick note: You don't have to use every one of these questions on every person you meet. For networking events, I recommend that you keep three or four of them available as conversation starters. Any more than that and you will be monopolizing their time. After all, they should be trying to meet people they don't know, too.

BE INTERESTED. LISTEN.

You're armed with your list of possible questions and are ready to take the networking world by storm. Great. I wish the next lesson weren't necessary, but I've seen too many people try to use these questions and fail because they neglect to practice one simple tactic.

They forget to listen.

You can't ask worthy follow-up questions if you don't listen to what they say. After all, you don't know what you are asking about.

Pay attention! The person you're talking with at that moment is the most important person in the room. Being inattentive to them (especially when they're answering a question *you've* asked them) is just plain rude.

The idea of listening brings us to a technique of the master networkers. My wife taught me this one. She uses it a lot in business meetings, but it works just as well in lectures, one-to-ones, and any other situation where we are listening to someone else speak.

The challenge is that most people will listen to what the other person has to say — and that's all. Don't get me wrong, we should definitely have our ears open to the content of the other person's words. To be truly great networkers, though, we need to go beyond the words and listen for the reasons *behind* what they are saying, because *that's* where the real person lives.

They're telling us about a new product that their company is marketing? Great! *Why* are they telling us about this?

- Are they trying to understand their target market?
- Do they need reassurance that the product is valuable?
- Are they looking for a referral? For what?
- Are they looking for clients or business partners?
- Do they need an introduction to someone who can help out in any of these areas?

Of course, since we aren't The Amazing Kreskin, Psychic Extraordinaire to European Royalty, we should go beyond attempting to intuit their underlying motivation and actually question them about it. If we think they are trying to hash out their target market, we might be able to help them by asking who'd benefit from such a product or to whom they would prefer to sell it. If we think they are looking for reassurance, we might ask about people who love the product already.

If we show a level of interest beyond simple information gathering — if we ask about more than the product — then they'll know that we care about them and their success. We're genuinely interested in them and aren't merely waiting for them to stop talking.

When we show that level of care, we shouldn't be surprised when they respond with a similar level of interest and respect.

CONNECT WITH THE PERSON

Ultimately, what these conversations are about is simply connecting with them as a person. They are not a prospect. They are not a business. They are not a referral source. The person you are chatting with is an individual with her own dreams, goals, and insecurities. Treat her as such and ultimately you will develop stronger and deeper relationships that will end up being more profitable in the long run.

ENDING THE CONVERSATION

You've become tremendously successful as a conversationalist. You can break in, break the ice, and ask great questions with the best of them. You still have one problem. You're having a tough time breaking away. Instead of meeting many new people, you end up chatting to one person the entire time and you aren't achieving your goals as a result. How do you get out?

We'll cover several techniques to help you do this, but before we dive in, I do want to insert a brief caveat:

Networking is a human activity. This means it doesn't necessarily adhere to a strict set of rules. Humans are notoriously messy that way. These techniques we're about to cover will work most of the time, *but* every once in a while you run into someone who is so socially clueless, you can hand him an engraved card that says **"Get away from me!"** and he won't take the subtle hint. That said, in the time since I've started using these techniques, I've never run into someone with whom they didn't work. Your mileage may vary.

The other assumption we are making here is that, while you do want to break away from this conversation, you want to do it gracefully. You don't want that other person to feel embarrassed or disrespected.

Here's a list of possible strategies you might use to terminate a conversation without making the other person feel like you are blowing them off.

HELP! I'M IN A CONVERSATION. NOW WHAT DO I DO?

1. **First, you can offer to help them.** "Bob, I've been having a great time chatting with you, but I feel like I've been monopolizing your time and I'm sure you have your own networking to do. Before I let you go, to whom can I introduce you? Who are you trying to meet?" While, yes, you are breaking off your conversation with him, you aren't leaving him completely high and dry. Even if you don't know the person Bob is trying to meet, you could still connect him with the event organizer who might be better able to help him.

2. **Next, you could ask for their help.** If you are at an event where you are the newbie, you can flip the process: "Sally, I wanted to thank you for spending time with me. I know you probably have your own networking to do but, before I let you go, I was wondering if you knew anyone in Human Resources here at the reception. Would you be willing to introduce me?" You are acknowledging her expertise and experience. You are letting her be the hero. You are also potentially getting a nice introduction out of the process.

3. **Third, excuse yourself.** Here's where you can use the "need to use the restroom" or "need to refresh my drink" explanation. I don't like this one because it *feels* like a blow-off and you are leaving them alone — not nice. Still, it's good to have in your toolkit if you need to use it.

4. **The next one is one I've heard about, but don't care for.** Still, I know friends who swear by it when necessary. In this case you quickly glance across the room and pick out someone you know. Then turn to your conversation partner and say "Tim, I'm so sorry, I just saw Barb Fox walk in and I need to have a quick word with her in private before I forget. Will you excuse me?" My main problem is that not only have you left Tim hanging with no one with whom to talk,

you've also told him that he isn't as important to you as Barb. Remember, the person in front of you is the most important person at the event. Besides, face it, the excuse you gave is probably not technically true anyway.

5. **Finally, you could schedule a one-to-one.** If you really have been enjoying the conversation and you think it would make sense for the two of you to continue your connection, ask them if they brought their schedule. Then go ahead and set up your next meeting. When you're done with that, most people understand that you will be parting ways for now.

One strategy I don't recommend is to try to terminate the interaction by asking for their business card — that is, unless you actually plan on following through and calling them later. Listen, I've been networking for twenty years now. I *know* that only one or two percent of the people who ask for my card will actually follow up. Still, when someone asks for my card, my heart jumps a little and I think, "They like me! They really like me!" At least I don't wait by the phone for them to call anymore. Even now, though, I feel a little disappointment when people don't follow up with me.

Asking for someone's card is a social contract in my book. Don't do it unless you are going to act upon it. You don't want to be the person who disappoints them.

You can choose from these techniques to exit the conversation gracefully or maybe you have a few of your own. The best of them show respect for the other person and may actually benefit them in the long run. Remember, what you want is to extricate yourself without harming the potential relationship before it's had a chance to start.

CHAPTER

15

GET AWAY FROM ME! DEALING WITH LIMITED NETWORKERS

"I don't believe in villains — just people who channel their energy in the wrong way."

~ Elizabeth McGovern

If you've attended a networking event in the past, you've met them. They are the deck dealers, the strong-arm sales guys, and the status climbers. They think they are attending the gathering to make good connections — to find their success — but the way they've chosen to pursue their connections can make them appear as the villains of the story. In reality, they've simply limited themselves. In trying to achieve short-term goals, they are giving up long-term benefits — and they don't even know it.

Now that you know *how* to extricate yourself from a conversation, next we need to talk about the characters you might meet who might prompt you to *use* your new skills. In addition, we'll cover what else you might do if you're feeling generous and really want to help them instead of just running away (if that's even possible).

> ### IN THIS SECTION YOU'LL...
>
> - Develop your positive attitude toward negative networkers
> - Learn a gentle finessed way to apply correction — when appropriate.
> - Examine five specific cases to keep under observation.

YOUR ATTITUDE

First, make sure *you* are in the right place. Oh, I know you've been paying attention to all the material we've covered and you are ready to be a good networker. What I want to prepare you for is what to expect from the people you meet.

I've been fortunate to teach about good networking practice for the past several years. My clients love the tactics for being a good networker at an event. Then they go to an event ready to practice what they've learned.

Not long after that I often hear that they feel let down. Apparently they run into a lot of other people who *don't* practice good networking. My hopeful students suddenly hate being the target of sales pitches, conversation hogs, and business cards forced into their hands. They feel embarrassed, too, recognizing some of the limiting behaviors they've used in the past.

How should we, as good networkers, deal with the fact that not everyone has progressed beyond a sales mindset when it comes to networking?

1. **Remember, good networking practice is what *we* do.** We aren't at the event to be judge and jury of other people's behavior. Pointing out where a person isn't acting in accordance with "Robert's Rules of Networking" ranks right up there with telling them that they're being rude or they're raising their children wrong. It's unlikely to draw

you closer. In fact, you'll be guaranteed not to deal with them face-to-face any longer. They *will* be talking about you behind your back, though. Focus on your own practice.

2. **When necessary, correct with subtlety and finesse.** Occasionally, you'd still like to try to connect with someone, despite their limited networking behavior. Develop techniques to deal with specific bad practices. Most of these involve breaking the pattern.

3. **If they do make a mistake — and they will — forgive.** Remember the old "let he who is without sin cast the first stone" concept? I'm guessing you haven't always been the smooth, confident connector that you are now. You might even have engaged in these limiting behaviors yourself. In short, if they hand you a card without first asking you, they aren't trying to be rude. It's probably just how they learned to network.

4. **If they can't or won't make a connection, let them go.** It's not personal. It's not a reflection of you as a human being. Not everyone is a good connection. For whatever reason, they aren't ready to add you to their network right now. Face it. If they don't return calls or emails, you wouldn't feel comfortable referring them anyway.

5. ***You* are responsible for the relationship.** If you find you are connecting with someone, whatever comes next is your responsibility. If we were living in a fair world, then, of course, they should be responsible for coming half way. Since we aren't, we have to make it *our* business to follow up on the connection.

How we deal with *bad* networking is a measure of how far we've come as *good* networkers. Think of it this way: The more you are able to see limiting behaviors in others, the less likely others will see those same behaviors in you.

GENTLE, FINESSED CORRECTION

A few years ago I was working with one of my coaching clients. Tom was a technical person working in the computer industry, just as I had been. He had been working with me on the basics of how to conduct himself at networking events and he felt he was ready to test his wings. He signed up for a local business mixer and attended when the time came.

After the event, we did a post mortem on his experience. In general, he felt good about his performance. As I mentioned above, though, he was shocked at the lack of networking skills in his fellow attendees. In particular, he told me about someone he referred to as a "drive-by card passer." This woman basically ran from person to person forcing her business card into their hands. While Tom was curious how I would handle the situation, he told me that his solution was simply to take her card, and then ask her who a good referral for her would be.

Apparently it stopped her dead in her tracks with a look of complete confusion on her face. Obviously, someone in the past had told her that you measured your networking success by the number of business cards you handed out. It had never occurred to her that she would be better off if someone took an actual interest in her first.

Without realizing it, Tom had hit upon the perfect response. Whenever someone is following a set pattern of unproductive networking behavior, we simply have to make a point to break that pattern. The "drive by" who ran across Tom obviously had never had anyone take an actual interest in her. When Tom did, her programmed limited networking failed her and an opportunity presented itself to find out who she was as a person.

Remember, the folks who are exhibiting less-than-successful networking practices are usually doing it without malice. They simply don't know any better. Whatever the reason, by breaking their pattern, you may have an opportunity to help them become better networkers.

THE ROGUES GALLERY: FIVE SPECIFIC CASES OF LIMITED NETWORKERS

I've warned you to look out for limited networkers but what does one look like? Before I tell you, remember that, despite my referring to them as the "Rogues Gallery," these folks aren't villains. They are being the best networkers they know how to be. We just need to take the time to see below the surface and do our best to set the good example.

By the way, this can become a fun networking activity all on its own — finding new limited networking archetypes — if you see any you would like to share, please send them to me at gpeters@ thereluctantnetworker.com.

That said, following are five specific cases of characters you might meet and some tactics on how to deal with them.

THE STRONG-ARM SALES GUY

The first (and probably the most obvious) is the Strong-Arm Sales Guy. He walks into the networking event with that "sales focus" mindset firmly in place. Anyone he talks to is immediately weighed, charted, and categorized as to whether they would be a prospect. When he locates a new victim, it's time to haul out his patented sales-probing technique. His goal? To make you so uncomfortable with your life that you want to set up a meeting with him (or even buy from him) right then and there.

When you run into him, at first he might appear to be a good networker. He will ask questions about you and your business and seem to take a real interest. At some point, though, his questions might start to feel intrusive or even make you feel bad about your-self. That's the signal that he's got you in his "always be closing" crosshairs and is planning to lead you through his sales process with one end in mind.

Of course, we know the fundamental networking rule he's breaking is that networking is relationship-based, not sales-based. Somewhere, sometime, someone told him to go to the Chamber breakfast and find customers. He may even have had an accidental success or two that reinforced his misconceptions — kind of like having a minor win on a slot machine can convince someone to keep playing long after they've lost more than they should.

By violating the "no sales" rule, he's not only becoming a pest to those around him, but he's hurting himself, too. For his fellow attendees, he's wasting their time. He's not in a position to be able or willing to help anyone else but himself. Personally, he's going to have a hard time developing the allies who might have gone out to sell for him and instead has to do it all on his own.

In this case, the best you can do is not follow his script. Break his pattern. No matter how often he tries to take you down the pain funnel, turn the questions back to him. Ask him about himself, why he's doing what he's doing, whether he likes his work, and what he likes to do when he's not selling widgets. He might just give up and walk away looking for other victims to pounce upon, or he might turn out to be a decent conversationalist and a good person whom you might be able to help in the future.

The one good quality about this particular personality is he's used to rejection. Even if your efforts to end the conversation aren't completely graceful, he won't mind. He's already looking for the next potential prospect.

By the way, don't think that all salespeople fall into this catego-ry. Sales professionals can be some of the best networkers. A few, though — often those who have been around for decades or are being trained by someone who's been around that long — never learned that networking is not sales.

THE DECK DEALER

The second in our lineup of usual suspects is the Deck Dealer. We mentioned her briefly before. This is the person who apparently thinks her networking success depends on the number of cards she hands out. At the beginning of the event, you'll see her running from table to table, dropping off one of her cards at every seat. During open networking she rushes from group to group handing her card to everyone present.

The problem with all this activity is she's turning her business card into the networking equivalent of "junk mail" — and you know what happens to junk mail, right? Yep. Right in the trash can. She's not really hurting people around her, other than being a momentary annoying disruption in a conversation. Beyond that, she's largely forgettable. In fact, that's how she's hurting her own networking efforts. Because she isn't taking the time to actually connect with anyone, no one will remember her at all. Her cards end up in the garbage, and she fades quickly from memory.

Fortunately, you know who she is as soon as she shows up. You aren't going to confuse her with a good networker. If you don't want to be bothered, take her card (she might even give you two!) and step back out of the way. She'll blow past you in a second and leave you to your conversations with more serious networkers.

If you'd like to help, do what my client, Tom, did. Stop her and ask her who she's trying to reach. Break her card-passing pattern and get her into conversation mode. She will probably be an energetic and enthusiastic networker — willing to put in the effort. She probably won't have a great network, though, due to the superficial connections she's made in the past. That's okay. You can set the example and be the first of many stronger connections she might make in the future.

Ironically, as you get to know her better, you'll likely discover that the whole deck-dealing routine wasn't even her idea. She probably learned it from her supervisor (whose networking skills come from an earlier era) who may still use it as a metric to determine whether it was worthwhile sending her to the event in the first place.

THE CYBORG

Number three on our list is the Cyborg. This is the attendee who might as well have had his electronics surgically implanted. He's wearing his Bluetooth headset at all times or his cell phone is sitting out in plain view on the table. He's either checking his email or on a call even during the networking event. You might even notice him jumping up and heading out of the room to answer the phone during the speaker's presentation (assuming he's aware it's rude to take the call at the table).

The problem the Cyborg runs into is the disconnect between how he perceives his activity and how everyone else perceives it. He thinks he's a highly connected networker who's using his time and technology to the fullest. Everyone else thinks he's plain rude. A conversation with him could be interrupted at any second, since the presence of his technology should tell you that you'll be treated as less important than any call, email, or text message that might come in.

My wife is a keen observer of human behavior. As part of her business helping companies apply for government contracts, she interacts with employees and management at all levels, not to mention decision makers on the other side of the table. Her observation: The more influential and important a person is, the less likely he is to be interrupted by anything. In fact, the common quality my wife noticed about high-level people is that, no matter what they are doing, *they are completely in the moment.* If they are having a conversation with you, that is all they are doing. They are focused and undistracted. To enjoy their level of success, they know they have to "Be here now. Be somewhere else later."

The Cyborg isn't an important person. He allows himself to be at the beck and call of anyone who has his phone number.

This is one of those cases where I'm not sure you can actually help. Maybe, if you've somehow become close to the person in question, you can come right out and be blunt about it — "Put that darn contraption away!" Otherwise, if you find yourself in conversation with a Cyborg, enjoy it while you can and don't take the presence of their technology personally. If they allow it to interrupt you, all you can do is vote with your feet. Smile, wave, and walk away. Spend your precious time with other attendees who understand that you have to be present in the moment and the person in front of you right now is more important than that phone call that *might* be coming in — at least for the next twenty minutes.

THE CHATTERBOX

Next in line is the Chatterbox. Usually this person doesn't even realize he's causing a problem. Unfortunately, you might not realize it right away, either. At networking events, he first appears friendly and helpful. He's more than willing to answer any questions you might have — regaling you with long personal anecdotes that illustrate the point at hand. The danger of this particular bird is that he uses networking events as a means of meeting his need for social interaction. While not intending to harm, he will feed from your precious time to the amount you allow him. If you aren't careful, he can back you into a corner and spend an entire Chamber lunch talking about his favorite topic — himself.

A few years back, before I had learned the techniques of gracefully exiting the conversation, I was at a networking event at a friend's business. It was the company holiday party and everyone was having a great time. My friend took a moment to introduce me to a young gentleman who was a new client for the company. We each said our hello's as my friend wandered off and then the young gentleman was off to the races! He started telling me about his company and the product they made. He talked about how his product was revolutionizing the industry, how it was going to transform everyone's lives, and how it was going to corner the market. Apparently his product also gave him the ability to talk without drawing breath... *for forty-five minutes!*

I thought I was going to have to gnaw my own arm off to get away from this guy.

Truthfully, the fact that he *wanted* to talk wasn't the problem. He wasn't trying to sell at me. In fact, he never even broached the topic of my purchasing from him or investing in his company. The problem was that I felt largely unimportant to the conversation. He just wanted to talk.

The nice quality about Chatterboxes is you can usually find out a lot about them without any real effort on your part. You do need to decide if the people you are chatting with would make good connections. Their problem is they don't know when to stop. For many Chatterboxes, it's not that they aren't interested in you. Their behavior is simply a nervous reaction to being in a stressful situation — being surrounded by strangers.

In any case, to deal with this person, you should at least have your "graceful exit" techniques ready. After all, you have to be the guardian of your own time. As a more advanced networker, however, you could use questions to keep the conversation going in the direction you want. Still, be aware that if they never get around to finding out anything about you (especially if you have a follow-up coffee or lunch), they probably won't make good networking partners.

LEVEL LEAPER

The final member of our limited networker quintet is the Level Leaper. The Level Leaper is a close relative of the Strong-Arm Salesperson in that she engages in conversation purely for her own benefit. In this case, though, it could be more than a sale. She might want an introduction to one of your clients, or for you to donate to her favorite charity, or to meet with your parents about an opportunity in their retirement years.

Of course, we should know the underlying reasons we are networking and setting goals for the event leads to success. The problem is that what she wants exceeds the relationship level she's been able to establish in a five-minute conversation. She probably wouldn't consider asking someone she just met at a party to come over and help her move. For some reason, though, she thinks she can impose on a fellow networker in a business-oriented gathering.

The Level Leaper's main sin is she wastes your time. Her insistence on focusing on *her* needs means that you probably won't learn anything about her *beyond* that need. She's actually more dangerous to herself. On top of wasting everyone's time, she ruins her own reputation. Everyone who talks with her will feel like she's imposing on them — inappropriately — and she shouldn't be surprised when people start actively avoiding her.

In fact, this excessive self-focus can lead to other, less-endearing behaviors. Level Leapers often appear to be "looking for something better." You might notice them glancing over your shoulder, ready at a moment's notice to upgrade their conversation partner, should someone more important come along.

As always, you can gracefully exit the conversation but, if you want to take the time to see if a real human being lurks under that limited behavior, you can break her pattern. Remember, in a majority of the cases, people have been blowing her off left and right.

The best way to break the pattern is to take a genuine interest. You might try some variation of, "Sally, I'd be glad to introduce you to my Uncle Herman. Before I do that, though, I'd like to get to know *you* a little better." Then start using your questions to find out more.

SOME PEOPLE ARE JUST JERKS

Please understand. When we talk about dealing with the negative networkers, I'm not saying that these techniques will work every time or that, deep down, every person you meet is going to make a good networking connection for you. Some people are just jerks and you can't do anything about it. All I'm saying is, you might want to give them the benefit of the doubt. After all, every networker you meet, including me, has acted like one or more of these characters. If we got better, then so can they.

CHAPTER

16

FOLLOW-UP ON THE PATH TO LONG-TERM CONNECTIONS

"Wishing to be friends is quick work, but friendship is a slow ripening fruit."

~ Aristotle

Congratulations! You've finished learning all the skills to make your networking a wild success. You don't have to do anything else to make attending those networking events pay off, right?

Wrong. And this is where ninety-five percent of networkers fail in their practice.

One of the fundamental rules of attending a networking event comes into play *after* the event is over. If you miss out on it, then you might as well have stayed home and not wasted your time or money.

The rule, of course, is that **you *must* follow up.**

Whatever result you want from your networking, it can only come from establishing those mutually beneficial, long-term relationships we first talked about way back at the beginning of Part 1. The greatest benefits stem from the strongest connections. Those connections don't happen five minutes at a time, once a month, in a crowded room. They happen in phone calls, over coffees, and during lunch.

And the first step is to follow up.

IN THIS SECTION YOU'LL...

- Learn why you have to follow up.
- Pick up some strategies on what to do with the business cards you collect.
- Discover a better way of doing your follow-up.

THE FAILURE OF THE BUSINESS CARD – WHY YOU NEED TO FOLLOW UP

When I started networking in earnest twenty years ago, I used to get so excited when someone would ask for my business card. The problem...what I thought was happening was not what they thought was happening. Here's what I assumed was going on inside their heads:

Oh, boy! I'm getting one of Greg Peters' business cards! I'm going to take it home right now and search through my contacts to find someone I can connect him with. Maybe I can hire him! Hey, maybe I should ask for two cards. That way I can frame one of them and hang it over my desk and then pass the other along to someone special in my network!

I might be exaggerating a little bit, but the bottom line is — and I know you are going to be shocked by this — no one *ever* called (unless they had a widget or service they wanted to sell to *me*).

Obviously my version of what they were thinking was woefully incorrect. What I suspect they were actually thinking could have been any of the following:

- *Seems like a nice guy. Maybe I'll call him.*
- *I can't remember his name.*
- *I'll put this on the stack on my desk and get to it as soon as I can.*
- *If I take his card then I can give him one of mine.*
- *If I take his card maybe he'll go away so I can go get some lunch.*

In fact, over the years I've done informal polling and a few casual experiments of my own. In general, my results tell me, the response rate when they ask for your card and then actually follow-up with you (without planning to sell to you) is probably around two percent. It's certainly not as high as ten percent. That rate drops even lower if you happen to be a deck dealer and hand out your card to anyone who isn't actively moving away from you.

What can you do to beat the odds?

Simple. If you want to talk with them again, ask them for *their* business card (whether or not they ask you for yours). Then, when you return to the office, *you* follow through. You have to be the two percent of people who actually **follow through with the follow-up.** Send them an email. Give them a call. Schedule a coffee. If you had a decent conversation, connect with them on your favorite social media site.

Just remember, someone asking you for your card does not mean that the connection has been made. At best it means that they are open to continuing the networking relationship; the next step is up to you.

WHAT DO I DO WITH THE CARDS I COLLECTED?

You've gone to an event. You've met and chatted with remarkable people. You asked for and received their business cards.

Now what?

I know for me, for many years, those cards would eventually end up in a messy pile on my desk that kept getting deeper and deeper. Eventually the clutter would drive me nuts and I would have to clean off my desk. To my horror (maybe that's a *little* dramatic), I would find that I couldn't even remember ninety percent of the people whose names and businesses were on the cards. I would reluctantly throw them in the trash. The remaining ten percent? I'd use them to start the new pile.

The problem was that I didn't have a good system for processing them — one that achieves the results I wanted from my networking efforts.

I'm guessing that you, too, have experience with this dilemma. Walking away from a successful networking event, you might have two or five or more cards in your pocket or purse from people who seem like good connections — people with whom you felt some amount of chemistry. Now you have to process them. Those business cards you collected don't do you any good unless you reach out to the persons behind those scraps of paper.

I'm sure even the best networkers have a few business cards lying around from people with whom they really meant to get in contact and it just never happened. The trick to minimizing that pile is to have a system that you use to follow up. That system should

1. **Be easy.** If it isn't easy to do, then you will never be able to maintain a habit of doing it.

2. **Be immediate.** The longer you wait the higher that pile of cards will get.

3. **Be personal.** Doing a form letter or email will actually work against your goals.

4. **Be specific.** If you want to set up a meeting with someone, come right out and say so.

5. **Be appropriate.** If you do want to set up a meeting with someone, probably a handwritten note isn't the mechanism you should choose. That takes too long.

6. **Be fun.** This is a tough one sometimes. Often this process feels similar to cold calling, which nobody likes. Remember, though, you are contacting them, not to sell, but to see if they would like to be friends. Tie in a small reward just for you when you have completed the task.

Over time, I finally came up with a system that worked for me. It's a fairly simple system. Otherwise I would never use it and we would go back to the "messy pile" plan. I call it...

THE THREE-PILE BUSINESS CARD SHUFFLE

First, I found a box. You could use folders, I suppose, but I have a real problem with "out of sight, out of mind" syndrome, so I wanted to make sure they were in view whenever I sat down. The box I chose was a small one that I had received with a sample order of my business cards. I then took some old business cards to use as dividers and created three sections: "To Contact," "Awaiting Response," and "To Record."

Here's how the system works:

1. As soon as I return from a networking event I sort all of the cards into two piles. Into the first pile go the cards of people with whom I really want to follow up. These are the folks with whom I felt some chemistry and I saw the potential where not only they might be able to help me, but I felt I had resources to offer them, too. On the back of these cards, I write an expiration date. The rule I use is one day for every two minutes of conversation — and never longer than a week. My reasoning is that anything longer and they've forgotten about me. I sort the cards by expiration date and put them into the first slot — my "To Contact" area.

2. The remaining cards are either people about whom I can't remember anything (usually the Deck Dealers) or the people with whom I don't really want to associate (usually the Strong-Arm Salespeople). These cards go into the garbage.

At this point, you might be gasping in horror. "What? You *throw out* those cards?" Yes. The way I look at it, if I can't remember or don't want to associate with them, what's the point of cluttering up my address book and my life with their contact information? I suppose you can do something with the information if you want (or if your company has a policy about it), but since I don't sign up anyone for my newsletter without their direct permission nor would I recommend someone I don't know, that card is just taking up space.

By the way, this process works with those existing piles of cards you have on your desk, too. I've had clients tell me how liberating it was to get rid of the unsightly pile (or piles) that were taking up their mind space every time they sat down to work.

The next part of the system is merging these cards into your daily networking practice:

1. Each day, take out a few of the cards from the "To Contact" pile and, well, *contact them*. Call them, email them, whatever works for you. If you promised to provide them with specific information such as the date and time of the next event be sure to include that in your message. Your goal is to get an opportunity for a longer conversation so you can look for opportunities to help each other.

2. If you weren't able to reach them but did leave a message (or just sent an email), they would go into the next slot, the "Awaiting Response" area. If you do reach them and are able to have either a longer connection right then or schedule a chat, the card goes into "To Record."

One caveat with respect to sending emails or written correspondence: Don't make them form letters. If your message could have been sent by anyone to anyone, then you aren't making a personal connection. That said, templates with the general structure of the message are fine, so long as you include personalized information that lets them know you remember who they are (and helps them remember you).

On a regular basis — once a week, once a month — the frequency is dependent on how many cards you take in — go through the files and purge.

1. Look through the "To Contact" pile. If you have stale cards — ones that are past their expiration date — unless you had a particularly remarkable exchange with them, you can probably just throw them out. They are unlikely to remember you. If you are destined to meet again, you will. Let it go.

2. The second pile, "Awaiting Response," may have a few cards in it. If they got back to you and you either set up a longer conversation or already had one, move the card to the "To Record" pile. Sometimes folks don't get back to you. If they don't, you have to decide whether they go back to the "To Contact" pile or into the trash. For me, that depends sometimes on the impression I received when I first spoke with them, or how many I already have in that first slot, or t might have to do with whether I'm in a grouchy mood.

Hey, I'm not a saint.

Before you make the effort to call them again, you have to ask yourself whether this behavior is likely to be the norm for them. If they aren't getting back to you, are they going to be similarly slow to respond to your referrals?

3. Your "To Record" pile requires a little more thought, but not too much.

    1. If you haven't had that longer conversation yet, then put them back in this pile.

    2. If you have met with them, then you have to ask yourself if they meet your personal criteria for being included in your network. Do you think you can help them? Did they at least show some interest in helping you? Did you have good chemistry with them? If they don't meet your requirements, again, let it go. They might not be in a good spot to form real connections right now. Throw out their card and leave space for those who *are* ready to connect.

    3. If you think they *will* make a good long-term connection, enter their information into whatever long-term system you have. Then make sure you reach out to them on a regular basis.

That's about it. It's not rocket surgery and you may already have a system that works better for you. For those of you who are still flapping your wings down here with the rest of the flock, though, you might want to give this process a try. It may help you renew and extend the connections in your network – activities that can only bring you more success in the long run.

THE IMMEDIATE FOLLOW-UP

I know with the Three-Pile system above, you might have felt uncomfortable purging the "Awaiting Response" pile. After all, you thought they might be good connections and you went to the trouble of reaching out to them. It just feels wrong to throw out all that effort. Is there any way to limit that waste?

Why, yes. Yes, there is.

But it has to start before you leave the event.

What if, at the height of your initial conversation, when you are both feeling excited about continuing your potential relationship, instead of merely asking for their business card, you ask them if they would like to get together for coffee (or lunch, or a phone call) at a later date? If they say yes, you pull out your calendars and schedule a meeting for the future. I call this the "Immediate Follow-Up."

When I teach this mechanism to my workshop attendees, we talk about the benefits as the "4 R's":

1. **Rapidity.** Calling or emailing people can take quite a while. That's time you could spend better in other aspects of your networking, your business, and your life. My wife once returned from a networking event with a pile of cards in hand. She timed how long it took to follow up on the potential contacts. By her calculations, she spent fifty-three minutes emailing, calling, and back-and-forthing. At the end of her efforts, she had managed to schedule (tentatively) *one* coffee.

   Contrast this with how long it would take to schedule a meeting if you were both standing next to each other with calendars out. Three minutes? I don't know about you, but I'd just as soon save that other fifty minutes for more productive pursuits.

2. **Reliability.** Here's where you get to avoid the "Awaiting Response" failure we talked about. Often when we try to schedule after the fact, we start out by playing phone tag or email tag. We leave a message. They call us back and leave one. We call them back, and so on. The problem is, often someone drops the ball — or someone's spam filter stops the conversation abruptly.

When you and your future networking partner both pull out your smart phones or day planners to schedule the meeting, it's hard for one of you to drop the ball. Oh, sure, something still *could* go wrong, but you've taken care of a big chunk of the potential problems.

3. **Recall.** Even when we are able to nail down a date, because of the backs and forths, that date can often be weeks or even months in the future. You might only have been face to face for a total of fifteen minutes. Now, you are showing up at the local coffee shop and all you can remember is that she had dark hair and her name was "Zelda." You are now forced to approach every single dark-haired woman to ask her if she's "Zelda." Not a comfortable place to be.

In contrast, if you schedule in each other's presence, you are likely to get a mutually agreeable date in the near future — far more likely that you will remember their face.

4. **Relaxation.** Even with a good system, acting on the cards you bring home can be a time- and energy-consuming process. You still have to make the effort to call or email them to ask for more of their time. If you follow the "Immediate Follow-Up" plan, the only cards that are going into the "To contact" pile are for those vanishingly few who don't carry their schedules with them.

As we talked about before, one rule of effective networking is to be ready with your networking tools at all times. Missing out on extending your network is like throwing your money away. That's why your calendar is the number one item on the list.

Get a scheduling mechanism, whether it's your day planner, your PDA, your smart phone, or the wall calendar your insurance agent sent you. Figure out how to use it, if necessary, and always carry it with you.

FOLLOW-UP ON THE PATH TO LONG-TERM CONNECTIONS

Whether you use the "Immediate Follow-Up" method, the "Three-Pile Business Card Shuffle," or other system of your own device, you must develop it into a habit. Only by following up can you turn those transient meetings into true networking gold.

CHAPTER

17 NETWORKING WHEN YOU'RE FEELING LAME

"Activity and rest are two vital aspects of life. To find a balance in them is a skill in itself. Wisdom is knowing when to have rest, when to have activity, and how much of each to have. Finding them in each other - activity in rest and rest in activity — is the ultimate freedom."

~ Sri Sri Ravi Shankar

All the techniques we've talked about are important and they will help you feel more comfortable and be more productive at any networking event you might attend. If you forget all of them, though, and only remember one idea, just remember that it's all about the attitude you bring with you when you walk through the doors. If you walk in radiating confidence and energy, people will be drawn to you. If others sense exhaustion, distaste, or annoyance, they will steer clear.

So the question comes up from time to time: "What if you just aren't in the mood? What do you do when the thought of meeting and making conversation with a bunch of strangers just exhausts you?"

NETWORKING WHEN YOU'RE FEELING LAME

As my final gift to you, until we meet again, here are seven ideas on what to do when you aren't feeling the magic:

1. **Fake it.** Yes, sometimes when you don't feel like networking, all you can do is muscle through. Put a smile on your face and a spring in your step. Walk in with your shoulders back and look for the lucky people who will be blessed with your presence today. Strangely, sometimes just showing up is enough to get you into the spirit. My karate teacher once told me that, while your attitude can define how you hold your body and the confidence you feel, the same is true in reverse. How you hold your body can define your attitude.

2. **Examine your intent.** One factor that leads to networking reluctance is putting pressure on yourself to sell — either yourself or your product. Remember that the goal of the event is to start relationships, not make the sale. Be aware of your "internal game." Are you listening to the devil on one shoulder reminding you that the mortgage is due or the angel on the other reminding you to find someone to help? Unfortunately, it's easy for us to slip into an unproductive focus on sales as a purpose instead of a side effect of the connections we create.

3. **Reset your goals.** Another success-limiting practice is setting goals that are too difficult to achieve. While I do recommend having goals that challenge you as a networker, you have to be aware of your capabilities in the moment. If you're tired or stressed, you might have to adjust your goals accordingly. Maybe instead of meeting three people, you should only plan on meeting one or two.

4. **Set "fun" goals.** Networking isn't — or at least shouldn't be — a grim, onerous task with only serious outcomes for every encounter. Sometimes it helps to remind yourself that

NETWORKING WHEN YOU'RE FEELING LAME

you can show up just for the fun of it, and set goals that are simply "for grins." I've done this before, especially at holiday or end-of-year events that are more social in nature. Instead of setting my usual "meet new people" goals, I decide to simply walk in the door, eat the food, and chat with friends. Ironically, it often ends up being a wonderfully productive networking event.

5. **Leave early.** In concert with setting an easy-to-achieve goal, give yourself permission to leave as soon as you accomplish it. Skip the lunch. Skip the speaker. As with exercise, consistency is far more important than intensity. You are far better showing up for five minutes and chatting with one or two people than you are skipping it entirely. You've still done your networking. You can go back to attending the full events after life gets back to a routine.

6. **Do other networking activities.** Remember, the event isn't the goal of your networking; it's the people you meet and the relationships you strengthen and extend. If you don't feel like going to the event, call someone in your network instead just to see how they're doing. You'll brighten the day for both of you. It's still networking.

7. **Skip it all.** If, in general, you're hitting ninety percent of your networking obligations, skipping an event now and again probably won't destroy your networking practice. Every once in a while, give yourself permission to sit back and relax. The danger shows up when skipping the event becomes your normal activity. To avoid this gap, simply commit to the next one. Maybe even invite a guest, to make sure you've got added incentive to show up.

Back at the beginning of this book, we talked about what it would be like to be a "natural networker." Understand that such a person

HELLO AND A HANDSHAKE   213

doesn't exist. Everyone needs to work on various aspects of this process. The best networkers have learned to enjoy the opportunities. They know that networking events shouldn't be drudgery. They should be opportunities you look forward to with anticipation. Be excited about the possibilities. After all, the next one you attend could be the one where you meet the person who will connect you with your next big contract.

Even better, you might meet a new friend.

ABOUT THE AUTHOR

Have you ever felt a little "reluctant" when it comes to networking? Greg Peters understands. A computer programmer by training, he was the original reluctant networker. Through study, practice, and lots of trial and error, he has been able to transform himself into a true networking professional, using the skills he learned to build a thriving Web development business.

Now, as the founder of The Reluctant Networker, LLC, Greg coaches individuals, trains staff, and presents to associations and other groups on how to get past their reluctance and start building better connections and stronger networks. He has served as the President of the Michigan Chapter of the National Speakers Association. He is also the author of several audio programs including "Calm, Cool, and Connected at the Networking Event".

When he isn't working with clients to help them discover the power of personal connection, Greg lives with his wife, two daughters, and two cats in Ann Arbor. He also trains in the martial arts, having earned his Master Black Belt in Tae Kwon Do.